CHANGING OUR APPROACH TO CHANGING THE WORLD:

Encouraging and Enhancing American Engagement in
International Philanthropy Through Tax Law Reform

For Lisa

CHANGING OUR APPROACH TO CHANGING THE WORLD:

Encouraging and Enhancing American Engagement in International Philanthropy Through Tax Law Reform

Joseph E. Miller, Jr.

COUNCIL on
INTERNATIONAL
LAW and
POLITICS

1st ed. 2013

Published by	Council on International Law and Politics 411 North LaSalle Street Suite 200 Chicago, Illinois 60654 http://www.cilpnet.org
Publications Coordinator:	Frank Emmert
Cover design:	Salma Taman
Cover art:	Cover photo taken in Gudele, South Sudan, by Barry Rodriguez. For more information, see www.barryrodphotography.com
Font:	Myriad Pro

Printed by CreateSpace

12 11 10 9 8 7 6 5 4 3 2 1

ISBN: 978-0-9858156-3-9

Table of Contents

Acknowledgments

One of the great ironies of academic writing is that while an author's work must be presented as his or her own, none of us truly can lay sole claim to ideas, conclusions, or lines of argument. We are created to live in community, and it is through community that our minds are sharpened, our hearts are tuned, and our will is prompted to express our thoughts and convictions to the world around us. If I were to give proper credit to all those who helped bring my mind, heart, and will to the point of articulating the message of this book, I would need a second volume equal in length to this one.

For now, I will content myself to thank those whose assistance directly and specifically shaped this work. In that regard, the book certainly would not exist without the guidance, encouragement, and editing work of Professor Frank Emmert, the John S. Grimes Professor of Law at Indiana University's Robert H. McKinney School of Law. As my academic advisor in the International and Comparative Law track of McKinney's LL.M. program, Professor Emmert was the first to suggest that I should devote my thesis to analyzing the legal framework of American philanthropy. He then supported my desire to augment that analysis with legal and public policy-based critiques of American philanthropy abroad, which resulted in the latter half of this book. As my thesis supervisor, Professor Emmert not only offered invaluable editing suggestions on content, tone, and focus, but he also proposed that I develop the thesis for publication as a book. For all of this, I am most grateful.

Ben W. Blanton, Esq., served as one of two additional readers of my initial thesis draft. Ben is my law partner and the most knowledgeable attorney I know in the area of exempt organizations law. Over the years, he has freely shared his wide and deep knowledge many times, and he did so again with this work by offering technical corrections and alternative ideas – always with the same generosity and graciousness that characterizes all of his interactions.

Jeff Pedersen, Ph.D., served as the other reader of my first thesis draft. As an educator and an experienced academic writer, Jeff's input was critically important in sharpening my focus and sparing subsequent readers from some of my most egregious and annoying stylistic habits (although some undoubtedly remain despite Jeff's valiant efforts). For these contributions, and for his friendship before, during and after the writing process, I am thankful.

Numerous friends and family members regularly bless me with encouragement, honesty, and models of selfless living. In the context of this project, I must give particular thanks to four: Lowell Haines, my professional mentor and one of the earliest proponents of my mid-career pursuit of an LL.M. degree; Jeff Jacobson, who composes a redemptive symphony each time he writes a book, an article, or an email message; Jeff Unruh, with whom every interaction leaves me feeling more alive and inspired; and Keith Carlson, who leads me and thousands of others – with his head and his heart – into lives of justice for the marginalized.

My wife, Lisa, has been my best friend and life partner for a quarter-century. Although I am far from a finished product, I am an immeasurably better man, husband, father, friend, and colleague because of Lisa's love, her encouragement, her desire to approach life as a cultural learner, and her willingness to share the learning journey with me. I now count our children – Grace, Sophia, and Josiah – as fellow travelers on that journey, and it is a joy both to teach and learn from them daily. During the writing and editing of this book, Lisa and our children gave me more patience, tolerance, and cheerleading than I had a right to expect – and for these gifts, I am even fonder of them than I was before.

All information herein is current and correct, to the best of my knowledge, as of March 2013.

S.D.G.

CHANGING OUR APPROACH TO CHANGING THE WORLD:

Encouraging and Enhancing American Engagement in International Philanthropy Through Tax Law Reform

We do not necessarily need to feel guilty about our wealth.
But we do need to get up every morning with a deep sense that
something is terribly wrong with the world and yearn and strive
to do something about it. There is simply not enough yearning and striving going on.[1]

Introduction: Crossing Borders to Bridge the Gap

Much has been written about the uniquely robust level of philanthropy in the United States, both historically and in a contemporary context. Individuals and organizations in the United States indeed have established long and deep patterns of benevolent giving throughout American[2] history. Such giving has been measured and analyzed innumerable times and convincingly supports the conclusion that Americans generously support charitable, educational, religious, and other worthy causes.[3] In 2010, for example, Americans gave nearly $300 billion to charitable causes in the midst of the worst recession in three-quarters of a century.[4]

American Philanthropy and its Legal Framework

As Americans' patterns of giving have matured, a vast system of laws at the federal and state levels also has developed to regulate, encourage, and even protect[5] the many actors who populate the universe of philanthropy: individual and organizational donors; charitable organizations; directors, officers, and trustees who govern charities; and numerous others. As described herein, those laws provide effective and comprehensive *regulation* of philanthropic giving in the United States, generally ensuring that

---

1   Steve Corbett and Brian Fikkert, *When Helping Hurts: Alleviating Poverty Without Hurting the Poor … and Yourself* (Moody Publishers, 2009), at p. 29.

2   Individuals of various nationalities throughout North, Central, and South America can lay equal claim to the term "American." In this book, however, the term occasionally is used merely as a convenience for the purpose of denoting United States nationality in a succinct manner.

3   The term "charitable" periodically is used in this book to include religious, educational, and other purposes described in 26 U.S.C. sec. 501(c)(3).

4   *See* Bruce R. Hopkins, *The Law of Tax-Exempt Organizations* (10th ed., John Wiley & Sons 2011), 2012 Supplement at p. 5 (citing *Giving USA* (Center on Philanthropy, Indiana University, 2011)).

5   For example, through civil immunity statutes designed to limit the liability of individuals who serve as volunteer officers and directors of charitable organizations.

charitable gifts are used for their intended purposes, preventing the diversion of dona-ted funds for private gain, and promoting the accountability of charitable recipients to donors and the general public.

At the same time, federal and state laws offer affirmative *encouragement* of phi-lanthropic giving and charitable activity by offering donors the opportunity to deduct charitable gifts for purposes of the federal and state income, estate, inheritance, and gift taxes, and by providing exemptions from federal and state income tax and certain state sales taxes and local property taxes to qualifying charitable organizations. Never-theless, such legal encouragements of philanthropy have their limits, and many of those limits may be found at the borders of the United States.

Stopping at the Water's Edge? The Need for More and Better International Philanthropy

American philanthropy does in fact stretch beyond the borders of the United States to support many charitable activities conducted in other countries. But such giving often is accomplished through gifts made to a United States charity that conducts or sup-ports charitable activity in a foreign country if the charity determines that such pro-gramming or support furthers the United States charity's own purposes. Less fre-quently, American private foundations make grants directly to foreign charities, and they do so only after completing onerous processes of due diligence to avoid prohibi-tive penalty taxes. Rare indeed is the charitable gift by an American individual or cor-poration directly to a foreign charity – not surprising, in light of the fact that under cur-rent federal income tax law, such a gift usually is not eligible for deduction from the donor's gross income.

The robust level of philanthropic activity *within* the United States is both en-couraged and well regulated by a mature system of federal and state laws. In this book, however, I contend that several well-placed legal reforms could encourage American individuals, corporations, and private foundations to complement their domestic philanthropic efforts with more frequent and more effective *international* philanthropic engagement.

In this context, I use the term "effective" to describe a learning-driven model of international philanthropy: an approach that places a high value on direction and con-trol by the foreign recipient while emphasizing a posture of learning and support on the part of the United States donor. This philanthropic approach admittedly reflects a normative preference for the primacy of the foreign recipient's judgments, preferen-ces, and objectives. Nevertheless, it comports with some of the most significant tradi-tional motives and objectives of philanthropy. Moreover, such a learning-driven model of international philanthropy furthers key national interests of the United States.

This viewpoint on effective international philanthropy also stems from my own experiences providing legal counsel to grant makers and charitable organizations for more than fifteen years. My perspectives on this issue have been further refined by my involvement as a volunteer in transnational partnership-style charitable ventures between American and foreign charitable organizations in international settings including South Africa and a Canadian First Nations reserve. As a lawyer and a volunteer worker, I have observed firsthand the enhanced outcomes – for the recipients of charity in other countries, as well as for American donors and volunteers who benefit from these relationships – when American philanthropy and charitable engagement is conducted with an emphasis on learning from indigenous foreign leadership. The learning-driven approach offers an alternative to traditional efforts that often reflect ill-informed presumptions regarding the superiority of American judgments on the appropriate use of grants and the methodologies that will best implement grant-supported programs.

While I propose basic policy arguments in favor of the learning-driven approach to international philanthropy, a full scientific evaluation of the relative effectiveness of the approach lies outside the scope of this book, which instead features more modest objectives. First, I seek to confirm through analysis that while the current system of American laws governing philanthropic activity is appropriately well developed for the purpose of encouraging and regulating domestic philanthropy, the system is less well suited to promoting effective international philanthropy by Americans. Second, I wish to summarize the most significant policy issues affecting American philanthropy (both domestic and international) while developing arguments favoring the encouragement of learning-driven international involvement by American philanthropists. Finally, I aim to investigate and advocate tax law reforms that would encourage Americans to make learning-driven gifts directly to international charities.

Many Americans discern a vast chasm between the way things are and the way things could be throughout the world, particularly in underdeveloped countries that face systemic poverty, disease, hunger, lack of educational opportunities, and myriad other structural challenges. Through several discrete and carefully circumscribed changes to federal tax laws, more Americans – including individuals, corporations, and private foundations – could be encouraged to play a part in bridging that chasm through philanthropic giving to foreign charities. The law cannot and should not mandate global philanthropic activity by Americans, but it can encourage more frequent and more effective "yearning and striving."

Overview of Analytical Structure

To provide context for the legal reforms suggested above, I first offer a survey of the existing framework of United States laws that affects philanthropic activity on both the domestic and international fronts. Chapter One thus begins by summarizing the scope of philanthropic activity in the United States and the breadth of the sector in which charitable grants are made. The opening chapter then offers a review of the various forms of legal entities utilized by philanthropists, as well as the state-specific procedures addressing the formation of organizations with charitable objectives. This background should provide a useful framework for exploring the connections between state-level legal forms and the classifications used in federal tax law to distinguish among various tax-exempt organizations.

Chapter Two explores the positive and negative impacts of various federal and state laws on general philanthropic activity. Following an initial overview of the policy rationales justifying federal income tax exemption, this chapter addresses the most significant legal regimes affecting philanthropy, including federal laws providing and regulating income tax exemption for charitable organizations; laws of general applicability governing the operation of charities, including federal-level reporting requirements, public disclosure rules applicable to charities, state-level regulation of charitable solicitations, and exemptions from state and local taxes; the important distinctions between private foundations and public charities, including the excise taxes and other unique rules imposed on private foundations; and the rules governing the tax deductibility of charitable gifts made by individuals and corporations, including an overview of the current legislative state of affairs as it relates to proposed deductibility limits to reduce the federal government's burgeoning debt.

Chapter Three turns to an examination of legal frameworks specifically impacting international philanthropy. In this chapter, I first analyze the general prohibition on the deductibility of gifts to foreign charities from individual and corporate income. The analysis then focuses on the detailed rules governing private foundation grants to foreign organizations, accompanied by a brief discussion of recent developments in the laws governing program-related investments by private foundations in the international context. Finally, Chapter Three compares the foregoing legal regimes to the equally detailed rules applicable to gifts made by individuals, corporations, and private foundations to intermediary United States charities that use such gifts to conduct or support foreign charitable activities.

Chapter Four shifts the discussion from analysis of legal frameworks to an investigation of the non-legal policy and practical issues that inevitably affect, and to some extent circumscribe, any discussion of charitable giving. In this chapter, I initially address general policy issues affecting all philanthropy, whether domestic or international, including an overview of relevant economic, sociological, and philosophical commentaries on philanthropic motivations. This general policy analysis also includes a discussion of the effects on private philanthropy of political and ideological views regarding the appropriate roles and limits of governmental responsibility for social services, the reality of persistent federal budget deficits, and the erosion of the tax base. Moving to a more specifically international context, Chapter Four next contextualizes the United States' role as a traditionally generous nation by studying the extent of international giving by Americans, acknowledging debates on the roles of government-sponsored foreign aid, and exploring the varied perceptions of American charities in other countries.

Chapter Five commences with a description of the learning-driven approach to international charitable giving, which accounts for the policy factors described above while promoting a mode of global philanthropic engagement that emphasizes a presumptive preference for local foreign leaders, rather than American grant makers, as the appropriate framers and solvers of problems. The balance of Chapter Five reviews literature across diverse disciplines as a backdrop for arguments favoring the utility of the learning-driven model, including (among others) its use as an effective problem-solving approach to persistent problems of poverty in under-developed countries, an incentive to innovation and risk-taking on the part of individual and institutional philanthropists, an encouragement of closer identification with grantees on the part of grant makers, and a means of protecting and projecting the national interests of the United States.

In Chapter Six, the discussion returns to legal analysis with a discussion of specific proposals for tax law reform that would promote the policies undergirding the learning-driven approach to international philanthropy. Chapter Six includes a critique of the recent proposal to create a repository for equivalency determinations that could ease the burdens associated with private foundations' grants to foreign charities.[6] The chapter and the book conclude with a proposal to offer limited federal income tax deductibility for charitable gifts made directly to certain foreign charities by American individuals and corporations. The discussion of this proposal includes a technical description of the requisite changes to federal law, a consideration of relevant practical difficulties and policy objections, and an examination of the methodological and technological tools (including the use of electronic equivalency determination repositories) that could be developed to implement such legal changes in an effective and responsible manner.

---

6   *See, e.g.,* Diane Freda, *Private Foundations Ask IRS to Allow Repository for Foreign Grant Information,* BLOOMBERG BNA DAILY TAX REPORT, May 2, 2012.

Chapter One:

A Brief Overview of the Philanthropic Sector in the United States

I.   A Profile of American Philanthropy

The United States boasts perhaps the most well developed network of philanthropic activity anywhere in the world. The sheer financial scope of American philanthropy is impressive enough: in 2010, approximately $291 billion was given in the United States to support charitable, religious and educational activities.[7] This figure encompasses charitable gifts by individuals (responsible for approximately $212 billion in gifts), for-profit corporations ($15 billion), private foundations ($41 billion), and estates ($23 billion).[8] Moreover, even in the midst of a national and global recession, giving levels continued to rise. A recent survey indicates that the median level of corporate giving increased by 7.4 percent from 2009 to 2011,[9] and overall giving rose by 3.8 percent from 2010 to 2011.[10]

Just as impressive as the giving data is the broad array of philanthropic organizations and endeavors in the United States. Poverty relief organizations, religious bodies, schools, hospitals, arts and cultural organizations, groups pursuing cures for diseases, animal rescues, civil society organizations, and many more weave a complex web of philanthropic activity.

The diversity and overlapping missions of such organizations defy any single succinct typology or taxonomy of the sector. Nevertheless, many have attempted to categorize and classify donors, charitable organizations, and fields of activity.[11] Part of the difficulty lies in nomenclature. Terms such as "nonprofit," "charitable," "tax-exempt," and "philanthropic" carry different meanings to different audiences, including (but not limited to) definitions set forth in federal tax law, state corporate law, and other substantive legal areas. Nevertheless, their usage often reflects incorrect

---

7   Hopkins, *supra* note 4, 2012 Supplement at p. 5 (citing *Giving USA* (Center on Philanthropy, Indiana University, 2011)).

8   *Id.*

9   Maria Di Mento, *Big Companies Slowly Increase Their Charitable Giving*, THE CHRONICLE OF PHILANTHROPY/THE GIVEAWAY (June 5, 2012), http://philanthropy.com/blogs/the-giveaway/big-companies-slowly-increase-their-charitable-giving/1997 (citing study conducted by the Committee Encouraging Corporate Philanthropy and the Conference Board).

10   Hopkins, *supra* note 4, 2012 Supplement at p. 5.

11   *E.g.*, *A Taxonomic Tree of Philanthropy*, CATALOGUE FOR PHILANTHROPY, http://www.cataloguefor-philanthropy.org/ma/2007/05_taxonomic_tree_of_philanthropy.html (web site last visited on March 3, 2013) (attempting to categorize donors and fields of interest in Massachusetts, as described in George McCully, Philanthropy and Humanity, 7 CONVERSATIONS ON PHILANTHROPY 43, 44-46 (Donors Trust, 2010)). *See also* Charity Navigator, "How Do We Classify Charities?" http://www.charitynavigator.org/index.cfm?bay=content.view&cpid=34 (site last visited on March 3, 2013) (classifying broad categories of charitable programs (*e.g.*, "health") and services and narrower "causes" within each such category (*e.g.*, "medical research" within "health")).

assumptions about shared definitional understandings, and they also are incorrectly used in interchangeable fashion.[12]

II.   Legal Context: Where the Philanthropic Sector Fits

In this book, I use the term "nonprofit" as a term of state-level corporate law and the term "tax-exempt" to denote organizations described in Section 501(c) of the Internal Revenue Code of 1986, as amended.[13] Indeed, commentators have correctly observed that tax-exempt organizations constitute a subset of nonprofit organizations,[14] as an entity may be organized for purposes other than profit (thereby qualifying for non-profit status under state law) without qualifying for federal income tax exemption. For example, an entity conceivably could be organized to prohibit the distribution of pro-fits, thereby satisfying the core requirement for "nonprofit" status under the corpora-tion laws of most states,[15] but if the organization is not operated in pursuit of any pur-pose described in Code section 501(c), it is not "tax-exempt." Such taxable nonprofit organizations are rare but not unknown.

The majority of philanthropic gifts are made to tax-exempt charitable[16] orga-nizations described within Code section 501(c)(3), which itself represents only one of over twenty different categories of federal income tax exemption. Title holding companies, social welfare organizations, labor and agricultural organizations, trade associations and business leagues, and social clubs are just some of the other types of organizations that are exempt from federal income tax.[17] Charitable organizations enjoy a preeminent position among this group. As explained in greater detail below, donors to such organizations may be able to deduct the value of their contributions from adjusted gross income, thereby reducing their federal income tax burdens.[18] Sub-sequent sections of this paper will analyze in depth the requirements for tax exemp-tion under Code section 501(c)(3) and the limitations and requirements associated with the charitable deduction, particularly in the international context.

---

12   *See., e.g.,* McCully, *supra* note 11, at p. 46 (discussing such confusion between the terms "nonprofit" and "philanthropy"). For more extensive discussion of the term "nonprofit," *see, e.g.,* Bruce R. Hopkins, *The Law of Tax-Exempt Organizations* (10th ed., John Wiley & Sons 2011), at 4-5.

13   26 U.S.C. sec. 501(c). Title 26 of the United States Code sometimes is referred to herein as the "Code."

14   *See* Hopkins, *supra* note 4, at p. 6.

15   *E.g.,* Indiana Code sec. 23-17-21-1, *et seq.* (generally prohibiting nonprofit corporations from distributing corporate assets to individuals and for-profit organizations).

16   As indicated *supra* in note 3, I often use the term "charitable" to include religion and education. This usage comports with the definition of "charitable" found in 26 CFR sec. 1.501(c)(3)-1(d)(2) of the United States Treasury Regulations. Title 26 of the Code of Federal Regulations is sometimes referred to herein collectively as the "Treasury Regulations" or "Treas. Regs."

17   *See* Code secs. 501(c)(2) and (4)-(7).

18   Different types of deductions are available for contributions to certain other tax-exempt organizations for non-philanthropic purposes. Most notably, for-profit organizations may be able to deduct payments to trade associations as business expenses under Code sec. 162.

III.   Choice of Entity Considerations for Charitable Organizations

When considering the creation of a charitable organization, among the very first important decisions to be encountered by founders and their advisors is the choice of
legal entity they will use to form the organization. This issue is one of state, not federal,
law; state statutes define forms of entity and regulate their formation, organization,
and operation. In general, founders have three basic alternatives: the unincorporated
association, the trust, and the corporate form.[19]

Unincorporated associations have fallen out of vogue in the charitable world for
much the same reasons as those accounting for their obsolescence in the for-profit
world: the lack of protection such associations offer to members and to individuals
who oversee and direct their affairs. While corporation statutes and trust codes
expressly provide limited liability – and, in some cases, levels of immunity from civil
suits[20] – for directors, officers and trustees, the individuals responsible for governing
an unincorporated association effectively operate without a safety net. Such individuals (and, arguably, the association's members) generally are jointly and severally
liable for the legal obligations of the association, such as contractual debts or legal
judgments.[21] Such unlimited exposure has eliminated the unincorporated association
from virtually all choice-of-entity discussions for founders of charitable organizations.

Historically, many individuals, families, and companies used the trust form to
accomplish their charitable giving. Trusts for charitable purposes feature trustees who
operate as fiduciaries of the trust's corpus, which in turn must be used for public rather
than private purposes.[22] Charitable trusts are relatively simple and straightforward to
form, as no specific language is required in the trust instrument, and it need not be
funded upon formation.[23] Nevertheless, the flexible nature of state trust laws also
creates uncertainty with respect to the interaction between trust laws and federal tax-
exempt laws. As discussed below, in recent decades nonprofit corporation law has

---

19   Limited liability companies ("LLCs") generally are not favored as vehicles for charitable organizations,
        as the Internal Revenue Service has observed that among other restrictions, all the members of such
        organizations also must be Code section 501(c)(3) organizations or government entities if the LLC is
        to be eligible for tax exemption under Code section 501(c)(3). Richard A. McCray and Ward L. Thomas,
        Limited Liability Companies as Exempt Organizations – Update, 2001 Exempt Organizations Continuing
        Professional Education Text 27, 30. Additionally, the "low-profit limited liability company" or "L3C"
        vehicle available under certain states' laws is not particularly useful as a vehicle for a charitable
        organization, in large part because federal income tax law does not yet recognize private foundation
        investments in L3Cs as "program-related investments." *See generally* William J. Callison and Allan W.
        Vestal, *The L3C Illusion: Why Low-Profit Limited Liability Companies Will Not Stimulate Socially Optimal
        Private Foundation Investment in Entrepreneurial Ventures*, 35 Vermont L. Rev. 273 (2010).

20   *See, e.g.*, Indiana Code sec. 34-30-4-2(b).

21   *See, e.g.*, Penina Kessler Lieber, "The Nonprofit Organization – Its Form and Structure," in Penina Kessler
        Lieber and Donald R. Levy, eds., *Complete Guide to Nonprofit Organizations* (Civic Research Institute,
        2005), p. 1-5.

22   *See id.* p. 1-10.

23   *E.g.*, Indiana Code sec. 30-4-2-1(b) and (c).

developed in parallel with the laws governing federal income tax exemption, and therefore state nonprofit corporation laws offer much more detailed guidance and regulation (for better or worse, depending on one's vantage point) than do many state trust code provisions relating to charitable trusts. While some founders may prefer such inherent ambiguity, in recent years the nonprofit corporation has become the entity of choice for founders of charitable organizations.

The Revised Model Nonprofit Corporation Act ("RMNCA"), completed in 1987, serves as the template for many states' statutes governing the formation, governance, and operation of nonprofit corporations. Indiana, for instance, revamped its nonprofit corporation statute in 1991, shortly after the RMNCA's promulgation, and its provisions on governance standards, conflicts of interest, and many other matters closely mirror analogous provisions of the RMNCA.[24] For those who seek to form a corporation for charitable purposes, the RMNCA's category of "public benefit" corporation[25] is the appropriate choice.

Assuming founders opt for the nonprofit corporation, the mechanics of forming the corporation are fairly straightforward and not particularly burdensome. An organizational or constitutional document must be adopted and, in most cases, filed with a state regulator of corporations, *e.g.*, a Secretary of State (or Secretary of Commonwealth). This document, commonly known as articles of incorporation, must be drafted with care to ensure that the corporation is organized and operated exclusively for charitable purposes, that none of its net earnings will inure to the benefit of a private individual or shareholder, that lobbying will not constitute more than an insubstantial amount of its activity, and that it will not engage in any political campaign activity, all as required by federal tax law.[26] Moreover, if the organization will seek federal tax classification as a private foundation,[27] its articles of incorporation must contain several prescribed provisions ensuring that the corporation will conduct its affairs so as not to incur certain penalty excise taxes that uniquely apply to private foundations.[28]

The newly formed nonprofit corporation must begin its operations through a governing body, *e.g.*, a board of directors,[29] who will assume fiduciary duties with

---

24   *See, e.g.*, RMNCA sec. 8.30 and Indiana Code sec. 23-17-13-1 on standards of conduct for directors; and RMNCA sec. 8.31 and Indiana Code sec. 23-17-13-2.5 on transactions involving directors' conflicts of interest. Unlike Delaware in the for-profit context, no state has developed uniquely protective nonprofit corporation laws to such an extent that it has become the domicile of choice for nonprofit incorporators.

25   RMNCA sec. 1.40(28); *see also* Indiana Code sec. 23-17-2-23.

26   Code sec. 501(c)(3).

27   *See infra* sections III(3) and (4) of Chapter Two for further discussion.

28   *See* Code sec. 508(e).

29   Many states now follow RMNCA sec. 6.03 in declining to require "members" of nonprofit corporations (members are analogous to stockholders in for-profit corporations, without the pecuniary ownership interest), instead allowing governance of the corporation by a self-perpetuating, appointed, or designated governing body. *See, e.g.*, Indiana Code sec. 23-17-7-3.

respect to the corporation.[30] The directors, in turn, generally adopt a governance document, commonly referred to as bylaws. The provisions of a nonprofit corporation's
bylaws largely reflect specific state law governance requirements, and they typically
address among other matters the selection of successor members of the governing
body; the proceedings of the governing body; the selection, duties, and powers of corporate officers; the formation and powers of committees; and procedures for addressing the corporation's dealings with its officers, directors, employees, and third parties.

Following the filing of its articles of incorporation with the appropriate state
authority and the adoption of bylaws, a corporate-form charitable entity generally
must seek exemption from federal income tax by preparing and filing with the Internal
Revenue Service ("IRS") an application mandated by federal law.[31] At this stage of
formation, it is critically important to develop an awareness of the panoply of federal
laws that govern the organization and operation of charitable entities, including those
that regulate charitable giving.

---

30   For a helpful overview of the nature and scope of fiduciary duties assumed by corporate directors in
        the nonprofit context, see Marion R. Fremont-Smith, Governing Nonprofit Organizations: Federal and
        State Law and Regulation (The Belknap Press of Harvard University Press, 2004) at pp. 199-211.

31   IRS Form 1023, Application for Recognition of Exemption Under Section 501(c)(3) of the Internal
        Revenue Code. This form has been developed by the Department of Treasury pursuant to Code section
        508(a).

Chapter Two:

An Analysis of Legal Frameworks that Affect Philanthropy in the United States

I.   Overview

Most philanthropic giving is directed to charitable organizations. Those grantees typically are exempt from the payment of federal income tax under Code section 501(c)(3). A discussion of the laws defining and restricting such exempt status, by itself, would (and does) fill multiple books. Moreover, beyond the laws of exemption itself, a vast array of laws affects the day-to-day governance and operation of charitable organizations and the individuals and companies who give to them. As one leading commentator has noted,

> Nearly all federal and state law pertains, directly or indirectly, to tax-exempt organizations; there are few areas of law that have no bearing whatsoever on these entities. The fields of federal law that directly apply to exempt organizations include tax exemption and charitable giving requirements, and the laws concerning antitrust, contracts, education, employee benefits, the environment, estate planning, health care, housing, labor, political campaigns, the postal system, securities, and fundraising for charitable and political purposes. The aspects of state law concerning exempt organizations are much the same as the federal ones, along with laws pertaining to the formation and operation of corporations and trusts, insurance, real estate, and charitable solicitation acts.[32]

In light of this daunting scope, the analysis in this book necessarily will be limited to the most significant laws affecting charitable organizations, with particular emphasis in Chapter Three on the laws applicable to international philanthropic activity. Collectively, Chapters Two and Three will address the following areas of law and analyze their impact on philanthropy:

- General legal requirements and restrictions associated with eligibility for tax-exempt status under Code section 501(c)(3);
- The unrelated business income tax rules;
- Procedural requirements for obtaining tax exemption;

---

32   Bruce R. Hopkins, *The Law of Tax-Exempt Organizations* (10th ed., John Wiley & Sons 2011) p. 3. The same author, in another context, has "marvel[ed] at the size of [his] book" addressing tax laws applicable to charitable giving, "[t]he very title [of which] suggests a subject that [intuitively] ought to be summarized in a pamphlet." Bruce R. Hopkins, *The Tax Law of Charitable Giving*, 4th ed. (John Wiley & Sons, 2010), p. xvii.

- Public reporting and disclosure requirements for 501(c)(3) organizations;
- State regulation of charitable solicitations;
- The federal framework distinguishing between 501(c)(3) private foundations and 501(c)(3) public charities;
- The unique rules governing private foundations;
- General federal tax law rules regarding the deductibility of gifts as charitable contributions;
- Laws governing, and in some cases prohibiting, deductibility for gifts to foreign organizations by individuals, corporations, and private foundations; and
- Restrictions applicable to gifts by individuals, corporations, and private foundations to United States charities for use abroad.

A basic understanding of these legal frameworks constitutes a prerequisite to any meaningful critique of their impact on domestic or international giving. Accordingly, Chapters Two and Three are offered as building blocks to support the policy analysis of Chapter Four, the policy arguments of Chapter Five, and the tax law reform proposals with which this book culminates in Chapter Six.

Nevertheless, even before embarking on a foundational inspection of the technical requirements for tax exemption, much less assessing the impact of those requirements on philanthropic giving, it is useful to consider why tax exemption is available at all. This inquiry is generally useful to a clear understanding of the legal regimes applicable to charitable organizations. A consideration of the rationales for exemption is particularly meaningful when considering the limits of philanthropic giving and potential reforms to address normatively grounded concerns about those limits (as will be discussed in Chapter Six).

II.   Rationales for Federal Tax Exemption: Political Economy Carries the Day

In the United States, we tend to take for granted the well-developed system of laws and regulations that grant preferential tax treatment to charitable organizations. The exemption itself, however, is not without its critics. As recently as May 2012, in a congressional hearing held by the House Ways and Means Committee, a prominent former aide to the Joint Committee on Taxation opined that exemption seekers should be required to make an affirmative showing of societal help, rather than simply demonstrating that they avoid the organizational and operational prohibitions enshrined in Code section 501(c)(3), which have served as the core legal requirements since the advent of exemption.[33]

---

33   Ben Gose, *IRS Urged to Reduce Paperwork Burden on Charities*, THE CHRONICLE OF PHILANTHROPY/TAX WATCH (MAY 16, 2012), http://philanthropy.com/article/IRS-Urged-to-Reduce-Paperwork/131899/ (summarizing remarks of Roger Colinvaux).

The most commonly advanced rationales for granting tax exemption to charitable organizations include the traditional favor with which Americans have viewed religious, educational, and charitable organizations; preferences expressed by Congress that reflect its desire to avoid taxation of certain endeavors on moral grounds; and exemption as a result of lobbying efforts by the charitable sector functioning as a special interest group.[34]

From a policy standpoint, scholars have scrutinized these observations from economic, political, and legal perspectives. Indeed, one prominent critic has suggested that the best justification for exemption is its compensation of charitable organizations for the lack of "equity capital" at their disposal (an argument grounded in the private inurement prohibition in Code section 501(c)(3)).[35] From this perspective, exemption offers a "subsidy to capital formation" for charities, and the subsidy is justifiable because for-profit providers are relatively inefficient providers of charitable services due to consumers' difficulties in making accurate judgments about the value of such services.[36]

Perhaps the most compelling policy rationale offered for tax exemption is grounded in political economy rather than tax: that the encouragement of charity through the granting of tax exemption reflects a desire to offer alternatives to government as a monopolistic provider of public services. This impulse, it is argued, is itself grounded in Americans' centuries-old skepticism of government.[37] From this perspective, the private sector offers variety, innovation, and efficiencies that may be absent if government were the only provider of charitable services. This rationale accordingly emphasizes the promotion of private charity as an expression of a classical liberal view of the interaction among states and markets. Such a justification offers fertile ground for innovation in charitable services and philanthropic giving, and I return to it in Chapter Six to discuss proposals for expanding the charitable deduction to include some individual and corporate gifts to foreign charities.

III.   Detailed Analysis of Laws Affecting Philanthropic Giving

1.   General Requirements and Restrictions under Code Section 501(c)(3)

Any legal analysis of philanthropy must begin with a clear understanding of the requirements associated with federal income tax exemption for charitable organizations – a category that includes many organizational recipients of philanthropy as well

---

34   Ben W. Blanton, *Introduction to Tax-Exempt Organizations*, EXEMPT ORGANIZATIONS AND CHARITABLE ACTIVITIES IN INDIANA (National Business Institute, 1992) p. 8.

35   Henry Hansmann, *The Rationale for Exempting Nonprofit Organizations From Corporate Income Taxation*, 91 YALE L.J. 54, 72 (1981).

36   *Id. at* pp. 67-68 and 74 (discussing "contract failure" in the provision of charitable services by the for-profit sector as a rationale for subsidizing charities).

37   *See* Hopkins, *The Law of Tax Exempt Organizations, supra* note 32, at p. 11.

as many institutions that engage in philanthropic giving. These requirements reside in Code section 501(c)(3), which contains four core qualification provisions: the private inurement prohibition, the exclusive organizational and operational requirement, the lobbying limitation, and the political campaign prohibition.

a.   The private inurement prohibition

Code section 501(c)(3) describes "[c]orporations ... no part of the net earnings of which inures to the benefit of any private shareholder or individual."[38] This passage sets forth the core distinction between tax-exempt charitable organizations and their for-profit counterparts: no private ownership interest may be held in a charitable entity. Stated differently, no profits may flow from a Code section 501(c)(3) organization to one or more "stakeholder" individuals or organizations.

The private inurement prohibition does not preclude the exercise of governance control over a charitable organization, which is distinct from the realization of financial gain. Accordingly, individuals or organizations may exercise such control through power to elect, appoint, or designate a majority of the members of a charitable entity's governing body (although limitations on such control of certain organizations appear elsewhere in federal tax-exempt law). In addition, this prohibition does not prevent a charitable entity from paying reasonable and necessary amounts, e.g., compensation (again, within limits and subject to certain exceptions established elsewhere), to individuals and others who provide goods or services to the charitable entity.[39] Rather, private inurement is defined in tax-exempt law as somewhat analogous to an equity interest. Perhaps the most fundamental expression of this concept lies in the mandate that upon dissolution, the assets of a 501(c)(3) organization must be distributed only for charitable or other exempt purposes, or to a federal, state, or local governmental entity (or by a court for redistribution to another entity for exempt purposes) – and not to "members or shareholders."[40]

b.   Organizational and operational requirements and the "commensurate test"

Code section 501(c)(3) also describes organizations "organized and operated exclusively for religious, charitable, scientific, testing for public safety, literary, or educational purposes, or to foster national or international amateur sports competition ... or for the prevention of cruelty to children or animals ...."[41] This two-fold test ("organized and operated") requires an examination of the organization's structure and an analysis

---

38   26 USC sec. 501(c)(3).

39   E.g., Broadway Theatre League of Lynchburg, Va., Inc. v. United States, 293 F. Supp. 346, 354 (W.D. Va. 1968) ("[t]hese things [goods and services required to carry out charitable activities] must be paid for").

40   Treas. Reg. sec. 1.501(c)(3)-1(b)(4) (this provision directly addresses the requirement of organization for exclusively charitable purposes, but it also reflects the private inurement concept).

41   26 USC sec. 501(c)(3). As noted earlier, the word "charitable" is used throughout this book as a shorthand description for each of the permissible purposes in Code section 501(c)(3).

of its activities. With respect to structure – the organizational requirement – the Treasury Regulations provide that an entity will be considered organized exclusively for charitable purposes only if its "articles of organization" (for a corporation, its articles of incorporation) limit its purposes to one or more of the purposes identified in Code section 501(c)(3), and only if such articles do not permit the entity to engage in activities that do not further such purposes "otherwise than as an insubstantial part of its activities."[42]

This slightly convoluted language – "otherwise than as an insubstantial part" – indicates that articles of incorporation may not allow a charitable entity to engage in more than a limited amount of non-charitable activity. Neither Congress nor the IRS has articulated any percentage test or other bright-line measuring tool for separating "substantial" from "insubstantial" in this context. In the absence of such guidance, however, the IRS effectively remains the arbiter of "insubstantial," and the most common settings for the exercise of this authority by the IRS are in considering applications for exemption, reviewing requests for private letter rulings, and conducting examinations or audits of charitable organizations.

As to the operational requirement, the Treasury Regulations specify that an organization will be deemed to be "operated exclusively" for charitable purposes "if it engages primarily in activities which accomplish one or more" such purposes.[43] As in the organizational test, the regulatory language elaborates simply by noting that the "primarily" requirement will not be satisfied "if more than an insubstantial amount of its activities is not in furtherance of an exempt [e.g., charitable] purpose."[44] Once again, the phrase "more than … insubstantial" is not capable of precise measurement, either by percentage of expenditures, staff hours, or other standards. Instead, charitable organizations – both grant makers and recipients of charitable gifts – remain subject to the IRS's oversight to ensure that the relatively inscrutable line of "insubstantiality" is not crossed.

Although it does not appear in the Internal Revenue Code or the Treasury Regulations, one additional doctrine bears mentioning in connection with the organizational and operational tests. In 1964, the IRS articulated the "commensurate test"[45] as a means of ensuring that a charitable organization deploys its tax-exempt assets to an extent that justifies its exemption.[46] This doctrine augments the operational requirement by reinforcing the notion that a charitable organization must primarily engage in charitable activities – not only by avoiding "more than insubstantial" amounts of non-

---

42   Treas. Reg. sec. 1.501(c)(3)-1(b)(1)(a)-(b).
43   Treas. Reg. sec. 1.501(c)(3)-1(c)(1).
44   Id.
45   Revenue Ruling ("Rev. Rul.") 64-182, 1964-1 C.B. 186.
46   Bruce R. Hopkins, "Law and Taxation," in Tracy Daniel Connors, ed., *The Nonprofit Handbook: Management*, 3d ed. (John Wiley & Sons, 2001), p. 914.

charitable activities, but by affirmatively engaging in or supporting charitable activities rather than accumulating tax-exempt assets and merely holding or investing them for purposes of capital appreciation.[47] This doctrine is closely related to the minimum payout requirement applicable to private foundations, discussed later in this chapter.

c.   The limitation on lobbying

To obtain and maintain exemption under Code section 501(c)(3), an organization must ensure that "no substantial part of [its] activities … is carrying on propaganda, or otherwise attempting, to influence legislation."[48] Yet again, this "insubstantiality" limitation is not expressly measured by statute or regulation, but in this case a quantitative alternative is available; most (but not all) charitable organizations can elect to have their lobbying activities measured by the mathematical rules established under Code section 501(h).[49]

Lobbying – "influenc[ing] legislation," in the language of the statutes and regulations – is defined in pertinent part as "proposing, supporting, or opposing legislation" by communicating with members of federal, state, or local legislative bodies, or encouraging members of the public to do so.[50] The federal regulations define "legislation" to include specifically proposed legislative action at the federal, state, and local levels, as well as public action through referenda, ballot initiatives, and proposed constitutional amendments.[51] As discussed below, private foundations effectively are barred from any lobbying activity under the taxable expenditure rules.[52]

The limitation on lobbying by charitable organizations is not without its critics. In his seminal work on private foundations, Waldemar Nielsen noted that the lobbying prohibition on private foundations has led in part to a general discouragement "from working in controversial areas and from playing the role of critic, goad, and pace-setter for government programs."[53]

---

47   In my law practice, I have often advised clients that the "reasonably commensurate" test is designed to prevent the proverbial tail from wagging the dog, for example, by tying up the vast majority of an organization's assets in illiquid investments that may grow in value but cannot easily be deployed in pursuit of charitable purposes.

48   26 USC sec. 501(c)(3).

49   Id. Code section 501(h) offers most charitable organizations (but not churches or private foundations) the option of measuring their lobbying expenses against their total expenses and sets forth percentage-based ceilings on expenses incurred for total lobbying and "grass roots" lobbying.

50   Treas. Reg. sec. 1.501(c)(3)-1(c)(3)(ii)(a).

51   Treas. Reg. sec. 1.501(c)(3)-1(c)(3)(ii).

52   Code sec. 4945(d)(1).

53   Waldemar A. Nielsen, The Big Foundations (Columbia University Press, 1972), at p. 397. Nielsen also notes with concern that the lobbying prohibition, along with other private foundation restrictions, implies "that there is something questionable, if not downright objectionable, about foundations that choose to work on social problems of great national urgency and controversy." Id. at pp. 377-78.

Nevertheless, the propriety of limitations on lobbying by 501(c)(3) organizations appears to be generally accepted, as evidenced by the absence of any persistent calls for the abolition of the limitation. Moreover, both private foundations and public charities may conduct certain legislatively related activities that are carved out from the definition of lobbying in the regulations.[54] These permissible activities, carefully circumscribed in detailed federal regulations, include, *inter alia*, certain works of non-partisan analysis and discussions of broad social or public policy issues, technical advice to a governmental body or committee upon written request, and so-called self-defense lobbying to preserve an organization's existence, tax exemption or core powers, or the continued deductibility of contributions to it.[55] This well-developed system of lobbying definitions, exceptions, and limitations offers an excellent example of the maturity of the United States legal system's balance between the encouragement of charitable endeavors and the establishment of safeguards against the inappropriate exploitation of tax-exempt status.

d.   *The absolute bar on political campaign activity*

The last of the four fundamental criteria for qualification under Code section 501(c)(3) is perhaps the most straightforward of all: a Code section 501(c)(3) organization may "not participate in, or intervene in (including the publishing or distributing of statements), any political campaign on behalf of (or in opposition to) any candidate for public office."[56] Unlike the preceding requirements, this one is absolute and involves no considerations of insubstantiality. The only significant analytical questions here center on what constitutes participation or intervention in a political campaign, and who constitutes a candidate for public office.

As to the first question, the federal regulations provide that participation or intervention includes oral or written statements on behalf of or in opposition to a candidate for public office.[57] With respect to the second question, candidates for public office include "an[y] individual who offers himself, or is proposed by others, as a contestant for an elective [federal, state, or local] public office."[58] Accordingly, a finalist for a gubernatorially appointed judicial post would not fall within the definition, and statements supporting or opposing such an individual's appointment would be permissible for a 501(c)(3) organization.

---

54   Although these carve-outs appear in the private foundation regulations, they "generally are considered applicable to public charities as well." Steven D. Simpson, *Tax Compliance for Tax-Exempt Organizations* (CCH, 2012 edition) p. 6016.

55   *See* Code sec. 4911(d)(2); *see also* Treas. Reg. sec. 56.4911-2(c).

56   Code sec. 501(c)(3).

57   Treas. Reg. sec. 1.501(c)(3)-1(c)(3)(iii).

58   *Id.*

Although charities are well advised to steer a wide berth around political cam-paigns, not all campaign-related activity is off-limits. Sponsorship of candidates' debates, for instance, generally should qualify as an educational activity benefitting the public, so long as the sponsoring organization remains neutral in its presentation and hosting of the forum.[59] Voter education guides also may be permissible, albeit within carefully circumscribed limits.[60] These clarifications again illustrate the effective blend between permission and limitation embodied in federal tax-exempt law.

e.   A note on "action" organizations

The federal regulations clarify that an organization cannot satisfy the requirements for exemption under Code section 501(c)(3) if it is an "action" organization as defined in Treas. Reg. 1.501(c)(3)-1(c)(3), because it will categorically not be organized and opera-ted exclusively for charitable or other specified exempt purposes. An organization is an "action" organization if more than an insubstantial part of its activities constitutes lobbying, if it participates in any political campaign activity, or if its "main or primary" objectives can only be realized through lobbying to support or oppose legislation.[61]

Importantly for the discussions of foreign grant making that appear later in this book, the IRS has ruled that for purposes of the "action" organization rules, advocacy activities in support of or in opposition to *foreign* laws also constitute lobbying acti-vity.[62] Accordingly, if efforts to change the specific laws of a foreign country (or sup-port of or opposition to proposed legislation in a foreign country) represent more than an insubstantial part of an organization's activities, the organization will be ineligible for exemption under Code section 501(c)(3) under the "action" organization rules. Arguably, however, general efforts to promote more effective lawmaking – or the rule of law generally – in developing countries would not constitute lobbying, because such efforts would not relate to specific items of proposed legislation.

2.   Other Laws of General Applicability to Exempt Organizations

In addition to the core requirements for exemption under Code section 501(c)(3), several other important rules apply generally to charitable organizations. For purposes of a general analytical overview of United States laws affecting philanthropy, among the most significant such laws are the unrelated business income tax regime, the procedural requirements for obtaining exemption, the public reporting and disclosure

---

59   *See* Rev. Rul. 74-574, 1974-2 C.B. 161 (discussing free air time provided to candidates by tax-exempt broadcasting station). *See also* Simpson, *supra* note 54, at p. 6004 (noting, for example, the advisability of ensuring equal speaking time for all candidates).

60   *See* Rev. Rul. 78-248, 1978-1 C.B 154, *amplified by* Rev. Rul. 80-282, 1980-2 C.B. 178.

61   Treas. Reg. sec. 1.501(c)(3)-1(c)(3)(ii)-(iv).

62   Rev. Rul. 73-440, 1973-2 C.B. 177.

requirements applicable to Code section 501(c)(3) organizations, and the state-level regulation of charitable solicitations.

a.   The tax on unrelated trade or business income

The operational test in Code section 501(c)(3) provides that no more than an insubstantial part of a charitable organization's activities may further a purpose that is not charitable or otherwise exempt.[63] This requirement, of course, precludes exemption for would-be charities that exceed the "insubstantiality" threshold, and it jeopardizes the exemption of those that already hold tax-exempt status. But what of non-charitable activities that constitute an insubstantial part of a charitable organization's activities? Federal tax law provides that such limited non-exempt activities will not jeopardize exemption altogether. On the other hand, they are not free of consequences for the charitable organization. Rather, such activities are subject to the imposition of the so-called unrelated business income tax ("UBIT").[64]

As a policy matter, the UBIT regime primarily operates to level the playing field between exempt and non-exempt organizations so that tax exemption does not merely serve as a competitive advantage in the form of lower costs for an organization engaged in commercial activity.[65] To this end, the UBIT rules impose income tax at regular corporate rates on the net income generated by trade or business activities regularly carried on by an exempt organization, if such activities are not substantially related to the organization's exempt purposes – and the generation of income to support exempt purposes does not suffice for these purposes.[66] The rules apply to virtually all organizations exempt from income tax under Code section 501(c), including grant makers and other charities described in Code section 501(c)(3).[67]

Importantly, when determining whether a trade or business activity is substantially related to an organization's exempt purposes, the eventual use of the income is not controlling.[68] Rather, it is the nature of the activity itself that must be evaluated for relatedness. To be substantially related, the activity must "contribute importantly to the accomplishment of [an organization's exempt] purposes."[69]

---

63   See the preceding discussion in section III(1)(*b*) of this chapter.

64   *See generally* Code sections 511-515 and the Treasury Regulations promulgated thereunder.

65   Treas. Reg. sec. 1.513-1(b); *see also* Carla Neeley Freitag, "Unrelated Business Income Tax," 462 Tax Mgmt. (BNA) Estates, Gifts, and Trusts, at A-1 (2009), pp. A-1 through A-2 (discussing Congress' attempt to curtail charities' ability to "expand their businesses using tax-free profits").

66   Code secs. 511(a)-(b), 512(a)(1), and 513(a).

67   Code sec. 511(a)(2)(A).

68   Code sec. 513(a).

69   Treas. Reg. sec. 1.513-1(d)(2). Interestingly, in light of the concern regarding unfair competition expressly stated in the regulations, the quantitatively measured extent of competition with an organization's business does not factor into the relatedness analysis. *See* Bruce R. Hopkins, *The Tax Law of Unrelated Business for Nonprofit Organizations* (John Wiley & Sons, 2005) p. 15. Nevertheless, the absence of competition may indicate that the activity is not a "trade or business" at all. *See* Treas. Reg.

In addition to the foregoing relatedness analysis, UBIT analysis also requires two other threshold inquiries: whether an activity constitutes a "trade or business," and whether it is "regularly carried on."[70] As to the first question, an activity undertaken for the production of income generally will be deemed a trade or business.[71] Thus, a proper analysis will investigate whether the sale of goods or services resembles the operation of a commercial, for-profit business.[72] Moreover, the actual profitability of an activity is not outcome-determinative.[73] Accordingly, a business does not lose its character as a trade or business for purposes of the UBIT rules simply because it generates a net loss in a particular year.[74] Whether a trade or business is regularly carried on depends largely on how frequently and continuously the activity is undertaken by the exempt organization, keeping in mind the underlying policy of preventing unfair competition with for-profit companies.[75]

The UBIT rules include numerous exceptions and modifications, many of which are designed to ensure that passive investment income received by charities and other exempt organizations is treated differently from income generated in an active business enterprise. Consequently, income from dividends, interest, securities loans, annuities, and royalties, as well as most rental income and capital gains, generally is excluded from the definition of taxable unrelated business income.[76] Nevertheless, if the property generating such income is subject to acquisition indebtedness, the income generally is subject to UBIT unless 85 percent or more of the property is used for purposes substantially related to the organization's exempt purposes.[77]

Not all passive income will escape UBIT. Rents, royalties, interest, and annuities received from entities in which the exempt organization owns more than a 50 percent

---

1.513-1(b).

70   See Code sec. 512(a)(1).

71   Code sec. 513(c).

72   *See* Treas. Reg. sec. 1.513-1(b).

73   Code sec. 513(c).

74   Of course, such a business may not generate any UBIT liability, because normal business expense deductions generally are allowed in calculating unrelated trade or business income under 512(a)(1). Nevertheless, if a loss-generating unrelated business activity were to constitute more than an insubstantial part of a charity's overall activities, it could jeopardize the organization's exemption under Code section 501(c)(3) and Treas. Reg. section 1.501(c)(3)-1(c)(1).

75   Treas. Reg. 1.513-1(c)(1). Certain activities, therefore, may be regularly carried on even if conducted for only a few weeks a year if such frequency typifies the conduct of business in the for-profit sector. *See* Treas. Reg. 1.513-1(c)(2)(i).

76   Code sec. 512(b)(1)-(3) and (5). A significant body of law has developed that analyzes the proper tax treatment of income streams associated with the disposition of intellectual property rights by exempt organizations. *See, e.g., Sierra Club, Inc. v. Commissioner*, 86 F.3d 1526 (9th Cir. 1996) (distinguishing nontaxable passive royalty income from taxable fee-for-service income and analyzing the extent of services provided by an exempt organization in connection with a royalty-producing contractual agreement).

77   Code secs. 512(b)(4) and 514(b)-(c); Treas. Reg. sec. 1.514(b)-1(b).

financial interest (*e.g.*, stock in a subsidiary corporation or profits interests in a subsidiary partnership) generally are taxable.[78]

Several other significant rules exclude certain activities from the definition of unrelated trades and businesses, including activities in which unpaid volunteers carry out substantially all the work (*e.g.*, bake sales and car washes), the provision of goods or services primarily as a convenience to students, employees, and others (*e.g.*, the operation of a campus cafeteria), and the selling of goods that were donated as gifts to the organization.[79] Another provision generally excludes specific activities conducted by trade associations and similar organizations at certain conventions and trade shows to the extent that the activities are undertaken for the purpose of promoting the industry's products and services or to educate attendees regarding new developments in the industry.[80] Even bingo fundraisers conducted by charitable organizations generally enjoy a carve-out from the definition of unrelated trade or business.[81]

Many other special rules pervade the UBIT framework, which even by the demanding standards of federal tax law constitutes a tangled web of cross-references, exceptions, and exceptions to exceptions. For charitable organizations making or receiving philanthropic gifts, perhaps the most important UBIT-related principle is the evaluation of "relatedness" by the nature of the activity rather than by the use to which income is put. Under this principle, if a grant maker operates a fast food restaurant, the fact that it will use net proceeds from its restaurant to fund a program of charitable grants does not render the restaurant activity "substantially related." To the contrary, because a restaurant business does not contribute importantly to the making of charitable grants, the net income generated from such a business would be subject to UBIT. Particularly in times of economic stress, when charities seek to augment diminished streams of donation income through alternate sources of revenue, they should first gain a foundational understanding of the impact of the unrelated business income tax rules on the income they hope to generate.

b.   *Procedural requirements for obtaining exemption*

Tax-exempt status under 501(c)(3) cannot simply be claimed by an organization that believes it meets the core legal requirements summarized above. On the contrary, nearly every type of organization[82] is required to apply for exemption from federal income tax by completing and submitting an application in the form prescribed by the

---

78   Code sec. 512(b)(13). Note that dividends are excluded from these "controlled entity" rules.
79   Code sec. 513(a)(1)-(3).
80   Code sec. 513(d)(3).
81   Code sec. 513(f).
82   Churches, a limited category of church-related organizations, and certain extremely small public charities (measured by annual gross receipts) are exempt from the application requirement by Code section 508(c)(1).

IRS.[83] If this application, designated as IRS Form 1023,[84] is filed within the legally required period,[85] then the effectiveness of the organization's exemption generally will relate back to the date on which it was organized (for corporate-form entities, the date of incorporation).[86]

The retroactive effective of exemption can be critically important for a new charitable organization seeking to generate start-up funding. Not infrequently, an organization must wait several months after filing Form 1023 before receiving from the IRS either a written determination letter evidencing its exempt status or a list of additional questions to be resolved before the IRS will consider issuing such a letter; in the latter case, the application process can be prolonged by weeks or even months.[87] The retroactive exemption rule allows an organization that has timely filed its application for exemption more effectively to solicit contributions during the waiting period from individual and corporate donors and, in some cases, private foundations, because the organization's tax-exempt status – if ultimately recognized by the IRS – will be deemed to have been in effect during the waiting period.

The application itself is relatively lengthy, and its complexity can, at first glance, present an intimidating obstacle to would-be exempt organizations, particularly those operating without the assistance of experienced counsel. Moreover, accuracy and completeness are critically important, for an organization's tax-exempt status will be based on the representations made in the application and any subsequent communications with the IRS. One leading commentator has likened the completion of the exemption application materials to "the preparation of a prospectus for a business in conformity with securities law requirements."[88]

The core of Form 1023 contains twelve pages, and it includes eight additional schedules, one or more of which may be required for organizations seeking particular classifications (e.g., as a school) or planning to conduct certain operations (e.g., the making of scholarships or other educational grants).[89] Among other matters, the application requires detailed information about an organization's past, current, and future activities; its compensation arrangements and other financial dealings with officers, directors, employees, contractors, and certain related organizations; and its

---

83   See Code section 508(a).

84   See supra note 31.

85   Currently 27 months from the date on which an entity is "organized," e.g., the date on which a nonprofit corporation receives its certificate of incorporation from a state authority. See Treas. Reg. secs. 1.508-1(a)(2)(iii) and 1.508-1(b)(2)(i); see also Treas. Reg. sec. 301.9100-2(a)(2)(iv), which permits an automatic 12-month extension of the 15-month time period specified in the Code section 508 regulations.

86   See Treas. Reg. sec. 1.508-1(a)(ii).

87   These waiting times reflect the author's experiences in submitting applications on behalf of clients.

88   Bruce R. Hopkins, The Law of Tax-Exempt Organizations Planning Guide: Strategies and Commentaries (John Wiley & Sons, 2004) p. 52.

89   These attributes are based on the most recent iteration of Form 1023, released by the IRS in June 2006.

fundraising activities.[90] Applicants also must complete a multi-year budget and a current balance sheet.[91] In light of the form's detailed requirements, accurate and complete preparation of the application constitutes one of the most onerous – and most important – phases of a charitable organization's formation process.

In short, Form 1023 is a lengthy, challenging document that can intimidate and even discourage individuals from moving forward with the exemption application process. Over the years, I have spoken with many would-be founders of new charitable organizations who find Form 1023 so overwhelming that they cannot imagine proceeding without legal counsel – and they often feel that they cannot afford a lawyer. Even some lawyers themselves are overwhelmed by the volume and detail of information sought in Form 1023.

With these challenges in mind, some leaders in the field of tax-exempt law recently have called for revisions to Form 1023. In June 2012, the IRS's Advisory Committee on Tax Exempt and Government Entities ("ACT") published a set of detailed recommendations for updating Form 1023, including a call to streamline the core form, a plea for the IRS to improve the quality and speed of its review process, and proposals for an electronic filing methodology and a web-based database of exemption applications (which are subject to public disclosure, as described below).[92]

c.   Public reporting and disclosure requirements for exempt organizations

A Code section 501(c)(3) organization is subject to several important reporting requirements at both the state and federal level. As a threshold matter, an organization must take care to preserve its status as a business entity in good standing under the laws of the jurisdiction in which it was formed by timely filing annual business entity reports with the appropriate administrative agency.[93]

At the federal level, several significant reporting and disclosure requirements apply to charitable organizations. These rules reflect an emphasis on the transparency of exempt organizations, and particularly charities that receive preferential tax treatment both in the form of income tax exemption and the ability to seek tax-deductible financial support. The key reporting requirement for charities lies in the obligation to file an annual federal information return, Form 990.[94] The filing requirement, which

---

90   Form 1023, Parts IV-VIII.

91   *Id.* at Part IX.

92   *See* Advisory Committee on Tax Exempt and Government Entities, "Exempt Organizations: Form 1023 – Updating It for the Future" (June 6, 2012), p. 2, http://www.irs.gov/pub/irs-tege/tege_act_rpt11.pdf.

93   In Indiana, for example, a nonprofit corporation must file with the Secretary of State annual business entity reports, containing updated information regarding its officers, directors, principal office, and registered agent.

94   Code section 501(c)(3) organizations that are classified as private foundations file Form 990-PF, which is not discussed in detail in this book.

may in some cases be satisfied by filing a truncated Form 990-EZ or "postcard" Form 990-N, applies to nearly all 501(c)(3) organizations other than churches, certain church-related organizations, and certain other public charities with revenue under a certain threshold.[95]

Form 990, "Return of Organization from Income Tax," represents both a financial reporting document and a tool for informing the public about the organization's activities. It constitutes perhaps the most effective means of maintaining accountability to the public and justifying an organization's continued tax-exempt status. Form 990, which was revised and significantly expanded in 2008, now encompasses twelve core pages and more than fifteen potential schedules, and it seeks information on annual revenue and expenses, program service accomplishments, governance policies, and the compensation of officers, directors, and certain employees, among other areas.[96] The failure to file Form 990 for three consecutive years constitutes automatic grounds for revocation of an organization's exemption,[97] and in June 2011 IRS utilized this provision to revoke the exempt status of over 275,000 non-filers.[98]

The scope and complexity of the newly revised Form 990 renders it challenging for many organizations to complete without the assistance of experienced and sophisticated accountants and, in some cases, legal counsel. To cite but one example, Schedule R to Form 990 seeks detailed information on "related organizations" and "controlled entities" of the reporting organization, including transactions between entities, which can require the coordination of return preparation efforts between or among multiple organizations.[99] Of particular interest to organizations conducting or supporting foreign charitable activities, Schedule F to Form 990 requires disclosures

---

95   *See* Code section 6033(a)(1) and (3). Nevertheless, public charities classified as supporting organizations are required to file Form 990 or 990-EZ regardless of their revenue levels. *See* Code section 6033(a)(3)(B).

96   IRS Form 990 (2011), Parts I, III, and VI-IX.

97   Code sec. 6033(j)(1).

98   Internal Revenue Service, *IRS Identifies Organizations that Have Lost Tax-Exempt Status; Announces Special Steps to Help Revoked Organizations* (June 9, 2011) (http://www.irs.gov/uac/IRS-Identifies-Organizations-that-Have-Lost-Tax-Exempt-Status%3B-Announces-Special-Steps-to-Help-Revoked-Organizations) (web site last visited on March 3, 2013).

99   For more detailed instructions on the required reporting of these relationships, *see also* Internal Revenue Service, *Exempt Organizations Annual Reporting Requirements – Form 990, Schedule R: "Related Organization" and "Controlled Entity" Reporting Differences*, http://www.irs.gov/Charities-&-Non-Profits/Exempt-Organizations-Annual-Reporting-Requirements---Form-990,-Schedule-R:---Related-Organization--and--Controlled-Entity--Reporting-Differences (web site last visited on March 3, 2013), and Internal Revenue Service, *Exempt Organizations Annual Reporting Requirements – Form 990, Schedule R: Reporting Related Party Transactions*, http://www.irs.gov/Charities-&-Non-Profits/Exempt-Organizations-Annual-Reporting-Requirements---Form-990,-Schedule-R:-Reporting-Related-Party-Transactions (web site last visited on March 3, 2013).

regarding activities conducted outside the United States and grants and other financial assistance paid to individuals and organizations outside the United States.[100]

Both Form 1023 and Form 990 are subject to public inspection.[101] This transparency requirement represents a very important fact of life for a charitable organization, for it means that the organization's financial affairs – including the amounts it pays to officers, directors, and key employees, and the amounts it spends on fundraising and administrative expenses – will be known to the public. Copies of Forms 1023 and 990 may be requested directly from the organization, in which case copies generally must be produced at cost[102] unless the organization makes the information available elsewhere (e.g., on its website) or can demonstrate that the request is part of a harassment campaign.[103] With respect to Form 990, identifying information regarding donors may be redacted,[104] and only the returns for the three most recent tax years must be produced or posted online.[105] For a number of years, GuideStar USA has compiled and posted annual returns for virtually all Code section 501(c)(3) organizations in the United States at www.guidestar.org. This electronic repository of returns serves not only as an effective tool for seeking financial information on charities, but it offers significant relief to charities themselves from the burden of copying and distributing returns in compliance with the disclosure requirements.

d.   State-level regulation of solicitations by charitable organizations

In addition to the federal reporting and disclosure rules outlined in the preceding section, charitable organizations are subject to tight regulation in many states with respect to the activities they undertake to solicit donations. Currently, 40 of the 51 jurisdictions in the United States require charitable organizations to submit some sort of registration with state authorities before undertaking charitable solicitation activities in the state.[106]

---

100   IRS Form 990, Schedule F (2011). See also Fred Stokeld, Exempt Organizations Must Report Payments Made to Americans Living Overseas, IRS Says, 64 THE EXEMPT ORGANIZATION TAX REVIEW 243 (2009) (discussing the requirement to disclose information on Schedule F regarding certain payments by exempt organizations to United States citizens living abroad or directors attending meetings in other countries).

101   See generally Code sec. 6104(a)-(b).

102   Code sec. 6104(d)(1).

103   Code sec. 6104(d)(4).

104   Code sec. 6104(d)(3)(A). Note that private foundations, however, may not redact such information from copies of Form 990-PF. Id.

105   Code sec. 6104(d)(2). For additional information regarding required disclosures of Forms 990, 990-PF, and 990-T (the return with which exempt organizations report unrelated trade or business activities and pay UBIT), see Hugh K. Webster, "Tax-Exempt Organizations: Reporting, Disclosure and Other Procedural Aspects," 452 Tax. Mgmt. (BNA) Estates, Gifts, and Trusts, (2009) A-1, at A-28, et seq.

106   See The Unified Registration Statement: the Multi-State Filer Project, http://www.multistatefiling.org/ (web site last visited on March 3, 2013). Of these 40 jurisdictions, 37 accept a common registration form, making registration a bit more streamlined for charitable organizations seeking philanthropic support on a national or regional level. See id.

In addition to general solicitation registration requirements for charitable organizations, many states – including some of the eleven that do not require general
registration – impose significant filing requirements on paid fundraisers or fundraising
consultants who assist charities in soliciting donations. For example, in Indiana, which
does not require a general organizational registration for charities seeking solicitations, each paid professional fundraiser and "professional fundraiser consultant" must
register with the state attorney general and pay an initial fee of $1,000 before soliciting
funds on behalf of a charitable organization.[107] Also prior to the commencement of any
fundraising campaign, a paid fundraising professional often must file with the state
attorney general a copy of his or her contract with the charity client, and the contract
must contain precisely prescribed information, including the amount the charity will
receive (which in Indiana generally must be expressed as a percentage of gross revenue to be raised in the campaign).[108]

The regulation of charitable solicitation by the various states represents a consumer protection effort.[109] Enforcement actions in Pennsylvania, for example, have in
some cases focused on shortcomings in the areas of fundraising registration, financial
recordkeeping, and the reporting of contractual agreements.[110] In general, these state-
level protections of the public focus on preventing fraudulent scams by telemarketers
and others posing as charitable fundraisers, as well as the assurance that charitable
organizations are not misused as vehicles for inappropriate private gain by fundraisers.[111]

e.   *A note on exemptions from state and local taxes*

Although the federal income tax exemption rules constitute by far the most important
exemption-related legal regime for charitable organizations, tax exemption laws at the
state and local levels also may apply, depending on an organization's activities and
property ownership. With respect to state income tax, state revenue departments
often use IRS determinations at the federal level as *prima facie* evidence of entitlement

---

107   *See* Indiana Code secs. 23-7-8-2 and 23-7-8-4. "Professional fundraiser consultants" include individuals
         who do not directly solicit on behalf of charities but receive compensation for providing advice in
         connection with fundraising campaigns. Indiana Code sec. 23-7-8-1. Employees of a charitable
         organization are not required to register or pay fees under these rules. *See id.*

108   *See, e.g.,* Indiana Code sec. 23-7-8-2(d).

109   In Indiana, for instance, registration and enforcement responsibilities lie with the consumer protection
         division of the attorney general's office. *See* Indiana Code sec. 23-7-8-1.

110   *See* Katherine C. Jewell, "When Charities Behave Badly: State Attorneys General on the Case," in Susan
         U. Raymond and Mary Beth Martin, eds., *Mapping the New World of American Philanthropy: Causes and
         Consequences of the Transfer of Wealth* (John Wiley & Sons, 2007), 277, 279.

111   *See, e.g., Madigan v. Telemarketing Associates*, 538 U.S. 600, 608 (2003) (Illinois attorney general's fraud
         action against a telemarketer did not violate First Amendment rights, where the telemarketer's
         fundraising contract with a Vietnam veterans' group allowed it to keep 85 percent of funds raised and
         the telemarketer "misleadingly represented that 'funds donated would go to further [the charity's]
         charitable purposes'").

to exemption from state corporate income tax.[112] As for sales tax, charitable organizations may be eligible for exemption from the collection of state sales tax in connection with the sale of goods in furtherance of their charitable activities.[113]

Additionally, some local jurisdictions offer charities exemption from the payment of real and/or personal property taxes. Because property taxes are imposed on the owner of property, however, complications can arise when the ownership and use of property diverge, such as when a charitable organization owns real property but leases it to a for-profit enterprise that uses the property for a commercial activity.[114] Indiana, for example, conditions real property tax exemption on three conjunctive requirements: that the property be "owned, occupied, and used" for charitable or other purposes that track those identified in Internal Revenue Code section 501(c)(3).[115] Similarly, personal property tax exemption in Indiana is available only where the property is owned and used for charitable or other exempt purposes.[116]

f.   Concluding thoughts on laws of general applicability

When considered in total, federal laws governing the conduct of unrelated trade or business activities, imposing procedural requirements in connection with applications for exemption, and mandating extensive public reporting and disclosure underscore the role of tax exemption in United States law as a privilege rather than a right. The laws require thorough, timely, and accurate reporting of information to obtain and maintain exempt status. Moreover, the regulation of charitable solicitations by statute and the enforcement of such rules by state attorneys general impose further safeguards against abuse by charitable organizations in the raising of philanthropic support for their causes. Finally, state and local exemptions from the collection of sales taxes and from the payment of income and property taxes often are coordinated with the requirements of the federal income tax exemption regime, thereby providing some measure of consistency to the three-layered patchwork of federal, state, and local laws across hundreds of jurisdictions.

---

112   See, e.g., Indiana Code sec. 6-3-2-2.8(1).

113   See, e.g., Indiana Code sec. 6-2.5-5-26(b), which grants exemption from such collection obligations to a category of organizations described in Indiana Code section 6-2.5-5-21(b)(1)(B) using language that closely tracks Internal Code section 501(c)(3), i.e., entities "organized and operated exclusively for religious, charitable, scientific, literary, educational, or civic purposes if no part of its income is used for the private benefit or gain of any member, trustee, shareholder, employee, or associate."

114   Difficulties also are presented by the reverse scenario, in which a for-profit entity leases property to a charitable organization. See, e.g., Hamilton County Property Tax Assessment Board of Appeals v. Oaken Bucket Partners, LLC, 938 N.E.2d 654 (Ind. 2010) (for-profit entity's below-market lease of a portion of property to a church, which used the property for its religious purposes, did not support property tax exemption for the owner).

115   See Indiana Code sec. 6-1.1-10-16(a).

116   See Indiana Code sec. 6-1.1-10-16(e).

These laws reflect the balance and maturity of the United States' legal system as it relates to the effective regulation of a sector that benefits from incentives and preferences granted elsewhere in the system. They impose significant compliance burdens on charities and their agents as a means of protecting the public from fraud and ensuring that the public's funds are actually spent for the charitable, educational, religious, and other purposes that justify organizations' exemptions from tax and the incentivizing of support from donors through tax deductions.

3.   Private Foundations v. Public Charities: Why the Distinction Matters for Philanthropy

When an organization seeks exemption under Code section 501(c)(3), it also must seek classification as either a private foundation or a public charity.[117] Unless an organization demonstrates its eligibility for treatment as a public charity, it will be deemed a private foundation.[118] It is difficult to overstate the importance of this distinction. Other than the deductibility rules discussed later in this paper, perhaps no other area of federal tax law carries a greater impact on American philanthropy.

Private foundations are subject to a host of operational restrictions and potential excise taxes in areas discussed in detail below, including (but not limited to) self-dealing transactions, minimum payout requirements, and prohibitions on expenditures for certain purposes.[119] For example, classification as a private foundation negatively affects an organization's ability to attract contributions from other private foundations.[120] Moreover, individual donors enjoy more generous deductibility allowances in connection with gifts to public charities.[121]

In light of the numerous rules that disadvantage private foundations, aspirants to exemption under Code section 501(c)(3) unsurprisingly seek to qualify as public charities if at all possible. Public charity classification may be obtained in one of three basic ways: (a) demonstrating a particular function of the organization, (b) satisfying one of two prescribed mathematical tests that measure the breadth of the organization's financial support; or (c) showing a requisite relationship between the orga-

---

117   See Form 1023, Part X.

118   Code sec. 508(b). Charitable trusts also may be treated as private foundations and subject to the rules governing private foundations. See Code sec. 4947(a)(1); cf. Laura Watson Cesare, "Private Foundations and Public Charities – Definition and Classification," 876 Tax Mgmt. (BNA) Estates, Gifts, and Trusts (2000), p. A-7 (discussing how charitable trusts may affirmatively seek public charity classification).

119   See generally Code secs. 4940-4945.

120   See Code sec. 4945(d)(4), which treats private foundation grants to other private foundations as "taxable expenditures" in the absence of the exercise of burdensome "expenditure responsibility" requirements.

121   See generally Code sec. 170(b)(1).

nization and one or more other entities that are classified as public charities under one of the methods described in (a) or (b).[122]

a.   *Functionally based public charity classifications: churches, schools, and hospitals*

Churches qualify for public charity classification based solely on their status and function.[123] It may be more accurate to say that churches are "deemed" public charities in light of the absence of any requirement for churches to apply for Code section 501(c)(3) status.[124] Those churches that do seek an affirmative determination of tax-exempt status must present evidence to the IRS regarding their formal beliefs, governance, membership requirements, ordination practices, schedule of services, and other characteristics.[125] These evidentiary requirements illustrate the IRS's views on what constitutes a "church" – a public charity classification that confers great practical advantages, including relief from the obligation to prepare and file the annual information return, Form 990.[126]

Schools generally also qualify as public charities.[127] The regulations indicate that this category encompasses "primary, secondary, preparatory, or high schools, and colleges and universities," and they do not distinguish between public and private schools.[128] Exemption applicants seeking classification as a school must demonstrate the existence and publication of a racially nondiscriminatory acceptance policy and statistics regarding the racial composition of faculty, the student body, and scholarship recipients.[129]

---

122   *See generally* Code sec. 509(a)(1)-(3). Other commentators describe these basic categories in various ways. *See, e.g.,* Bruce R. Hopkins and Jody Blazek, *Private Foundations: Tax Law and Compliance,* 3d ed. (John Wiley & Sons, 2008), p. 598 (describing the categories as "the *public* institutions, the *publicly supported* charitable organizations, [and] the *supporting* organizations)" (emphases added). Governmental units described in Code sec. 170(c)(1) also are treated as public charities. *See* Code sec. 170(b)(1)(A)(v). Moreover, organizations organized and operated to support state universities generally qualify as public charities under Code sec. 170(b)(1)(A)(iv), and an organization testing for public safety may qualify as a public charity under Code sec. 509(a)(4).

123   Code secs. 509(a)(1) and 170(b)(1)(A)(i). The latter provision also references "convention[s] or association[s] of churches" such as denominational groups.

124   *See* Code section 508(c)(1)(A), discussed *supra* at note 82 and the accompanying text.

125   *See* Form 1023, Schedule A.

126   *See* Code sec. 6033(a)(3)(A)(i), discussed *supra* at note 95 and the accompanying text.

127   Code secs. 509(a)(1) and 170(b)(1)(A)(ii). The latter provision describes "an educational organization which normally maintains a regular faculty and curriculum and normally has a regularly enrolled body of pupils or students in attendance at the place where its educational activities are regularly carried on."

128   Treas. Reg. sec. 1.170A-9(c)(1).

129   *See* Form 1023, Schedule B.

Hospitals and medical research organizations comprise a third functional cate gory of public charities.[130] Such entities operate under significant operational restrictions, which are enumerated in the federal regulations.[131] The federal exemption application requires hospital applicants to show substantial evidence regarding their provision of care to indigent patients, emergency room services, board governance, provision of office space to private physicians, extent of participation in joint ventures, and numerous other matters.[132] These organizational and operational requirements help distinguish tax-exempt hospitals from their for-profit counterparts.

b.   Organizations demonstrating broad public support

In addition to the functionally based categories described above, a Code section 501(c)(3) organization may obtain classification as a public charity, rather than a private foundation, by demonstrating a sufficiently broad base of public support. The Code and the Treasury Regulations describe two alternative public support tests. One test addresses entities that primarily receive their support through donated funds, while the other is more suited to organizations that generate revenues primarily through fees received for the performance of charitable or other tax-exempt activities.[133]

The first public support test requires an organization to demonstrate that it "normally receives a substantial part of its support ... from a governmental unit ... or from direct or indirect contributions from the general public."[134] This test generally is applied to an organization by measuring its financial support over its current and four most recent tax years[135] to determine whether at least 33 1/3 percent of such support is derived from governments or the general public.[136] While the regulations governing the calculation of an organization's public support percentage are numerous and detailed, they can be collectively described as a system for ensuring that a public charity

---

130   Code secs. 509(a)(1) and 170(b)(1)(A)(iii). The latter provision describes "an organization the principal purpose or functions of which are the providing of medical or hospital care or medical education or medical research ...."

131   Treas. Reg. sec. 1.170A-9(d).

132   *See* Form 1023, Schedule C.

133   The first category of publicly supported public charities includes most community foundations, which generally aggregate funds donated by many different individuals and organizations. If certain tax law requirements are met, the multiple funds held by a community foundation will be treated as a single entity rather than as separate private foundations. For an overview of the "single entity" requirements *see* Christopher R. Hoyt, *Legal Compendium for Community Foundations* (Council on Foundations, 1991), pp. 4-10.

134   Code sec. 170(b)(1)(A)(vi).

135   *See* Treas. Reg. sec. 1.170A-9(f)(4).

136   *See* Treas. Reg. sec. 1.170A-9(f)(2). The IRS also may permit continued public charity classifications for organizations whose public support level falls below 33 1/3 percent, but remains at or above ten percent, based on a consideration of relevant facts and circumstances. *See* Treas. Reg. sec. 1.170A-9(f)(3).

is broadly financially supported by a wide base of contributors, rather than receiving concentrated support from one or a few donors.

The most significant such rules include the following: (i) contributions received from governmental units and other publicly supported public charities (or other public charities treated as such) generally may be included in full in the numerator and denominator of the public support fraction;[137] (ii) contributions from any other discrete source (e.g., individuals, corporations, private foundations) may be included in the numerator only to the extent that the total contributions from any one such source (together with certain related parties) does not exceed two percent of the organization's total financial support over the measuring period, but they must be included in full in the denominator;[138] (iii) investment income and unrelated trade or business income may not be included in the numerator but must be included in the denominator;[139] (iv) receipts from the performance of activities related to the organization's exempt purposes are excluded from the numerator and the denominator;[140] and (v) certain "unusual grants" also may be excluded from both the numerator and the denominator.[141]

The second public support test, used by entities whose revenue primarily represents fees for the performance of charitable activities,[142] requires an organization "normally [to receive] more than one-third of its support in each taxable year" from a combination of gifts, grants, membership dues, and receipts from the performance of exempt services, all subject to limitations based on the source of such income, while "normally [receiving] not more than one-third of its support in each taxable year" from a combination of investment income and unrelated trade or business income.[143] The measurement generally must be performed annually for the organization's current and four most recent tax years.[144] Although the rules governing the calculations under this test are voluminous, the most significant ones include these: (i) gifts, grants, contributions, and membership dues from a single source must be included in full in the denominator of the public support fraction, but they generally may be included in the numerator only if all income from that particular source (together with certain related

---

137   *See* Treas. Reg. sec. 1.170A-9(f)(6)(v). Contributions received from churches that are publicly supported are treated as contributions from publicly supported public charities for purposes of this rule, and such contributions therefore may be included in full in the numerator and denominator of the public support fraction. *See* Rev. Rul. 78-95, 1978-1 C.B. 71.

138   *See* Treas. Reg. sec. 1.170A-9(f)(6)(i).

139   *See* Treas. Reg. sec. 1.170A-9(f)(7)(i), which includes in the definition of "support" any gross investment income described in Code sec. 509(d)(4). Such investment income is not included in the definition of public support in Treas. Reg. sec. 1.170A-9(f)(3).

140   *See* Treas. Reg. sec. 1.170A-9(f)(7)(i)(A).

141   *See* Treas. Reg. sec. 1.170A-9(f)(6)(ii).

142   Some museums, symphonies, and community theaters, for example, may meet this test through memberships, admissions, and performance ticket sales to the general public.

143   Code sec. 509(a)(2)(A).

144   *See* Treas. Reg. sec. 1.509(a)-3(c)(1)(i).

parties) constitutes no more than two percent of the organization's revenue since inception;[145] and (ii) receipts from a single source from the performance of charitable or other exempt activities must be included in full in the denominator, but they generally may be included in the numerator only to the extent that they do not exceed the greater of $5,000 or one percent of the organization's revenue in a particular tax year.[146]

These two public support tests carry the highest importance for public charities seeking philanthropic support. Maintaining the requisite level of public support under the applicable test will ensure the organization's ability to offer the more favorable deductibility limits to prospective individual donors.[147] Furthermore, an organization seeking a grant from a private foundation first may need to convince the private foundation that such a grant would not cause its public support to dip below the permissible level, thereby "tipping" the grantee into private foundation classification and causing the private foundation to make a prohibited taxable expenditure.[148] Accordingly, a manager of a publicly supported public charity must maintain constant awareness of the organization's public support level and the likely effects on public support of any proposed gift, grant, or other new source of income.

c.   *Supporting organizations*

The final category of public charities includes organizations whose ability to avoid private foundation status rests not on their broad base of public support but on their relationships with other public charities. For example, some universities are supported by foundations that qualify for public charity classification as such "supporting organizations." Similar entities exist in relationship to many other types of public-serving organizations such as hospitals and providers of social services. A supporting organization sometimes is formed in part for the purpose of segregating an organization's high-value assets from its high-risk activities, thereby minimizing the liability exposure of such assets (*e.g.*, land and buildings) as a result of the risks associated with the "supported" organization's activities.

A supporting organization is not required to meet a public support test. Rather, it must satisfy three statutory requirements: (i) it must be organized and operated

---

145   *See* Code sec. 509(a)(2)(A), which describes such support from "disqualified persons." Note that in this calculation, *all* revenue from such a disqualified person is excluded from the numerator, not just the amount above the two percent threshold (as under Code sec. 170(b)(1)(A)(vi)). Grant income from governmental units and certain public charities, however, is not subject to this limitation. *See* Code sec. 509(a)(2)(A) and Treas. Reg. sec. 1.509(a)-3(g) (distinguishing grants from fee-for-service income).

146   Code sec. 509(a)(2)(A)(ii).

147   *See* Code sec. 170(b)(1), which sets forth individual deductibility "ceilings," as a percentage of adjusted gross income, that are higher for gifts to public charities than for gifts to private foundations.

148   As explained later in this chapter, private foundations essentially are prohibited under Code section 4945(d)(4) from making grants to most other private foundations unless they exercise "expenditure responsibility" under Code section 4945(h).

exclusively to further the purposes of one or more public charities described in Code sections 509(a)(1) or 509(a)(2) (its "supported organizations");[149] (ii) it must satisfy one of three enumerated types of relational tests with its supported organizations,[150] the most common of which requires the supported organizations to control the supporting organization by, for example, collectively appointing a majority of the members of the supporting organization's governing body;[151] and (iii) it must not be controlled directly or indirectly by "disqualified persons," a term that includes, among others, substantial contributors to the supporting organization and other parties related to such contributors.[152]

The most obvious advantage of public charity classification as a "supporting organization" is the absence of any public support requirement. A supporting organization therefore has a greater degree of flexibility, in absolute mathematical terms, in accepting a large grant from a single source.[153] Conversely, the most significant limiting factors associated with such a classification include the requirement of a certain relationship between the supporting and supported organization(s)[154] and the fact that all the supporting organization's activities must somehow further the purposes of one or more of its supported organizations.[155]

The supporting organization form sometimes is offered as an alternative to private foundation classification to avoid the payout requirement and other limitations imposed on private foundations, although the prohibition on control by disqualified persons fundamentally limits the extent of control that can be exercised by founders of supporting organizations (other than the public charities themselves).[156] Impor-

---

149   See Code sec. 509(a)(3)(A). The category of permitted "supported organizations" also includes Code section 501(c)(4), (5), or (6) organizations that meet the public support test described in Code section 509(a)(2). See the "flush left" text in Code sec. 509(a)(3).

150   See Code sec. 509(a)(3)(B).

151   See Code sec. 509(a)(3)(B)(i) and Treas. Reg. sec. 1.509(a)-4(g)(i).

152   See Code secs. 509(a)(3)(C) and 4946. The prohibited control group expressly does not include the supported public charities themselves. See Code sec. 509(a)(3)(C).

153   Strict controls exist, however, that essentially prohibit grants by a private foundation to certain "Type III" supporting organizations, to supporting organizations that are controlled by "disqualified persons" (including officers, directors, substantial contributors, and certain family members of the foregoing) of the private foundations, and to supporting organizations one or more of the supported organizations of which are controlled by such disqualified persons. See Code sec. 4945(d)(4)(A)(ii) (categorizing such grants as impermissible "taxable expenditures") and Code sec. 4942(g)(4)(A) (excluding such grants from the definition of "qualifying distributions" for purposes of the minimum payout rule applicable to private foundations).

154   See Treas. Reg. sec. 1.509(a)-4(f). The preferred "Type I" relationship requires operation, supervision, or control by the supported organizations as described in Treas. Reg. sec. 1.509(a)-4(g).

155   To meet this requirement, "[a] supporting organization is not required to pay over its income to the publicly supported organizations." Instead, it may undertake activities or programs that benefit its supported organizations. Treas. Reg. sec. 1.509(a)-4(e)(2).

156   See Bruce R. Hopkins and Jody Blazek, The Legal Answer Book for Private Foundations (John Wiley & Sons, 2002) pp. 245-46.

tantly, Congress and the IRS historically have scrutinized the supporting organization form and its potential for abuse by founders seeking to exercise impermissible control over the organization.[157]

Another alternative to private foundation classification is the formation of a donor-advised fund within an existing public charity.[158] The donor-advised fund approach eliminates the need to create a new legal entity and lowers other administrative burdens such as the need to file annual returns for an independent entity. Donor-advised funds themselves, however, are subject to significant restrictions on management and expenditures,[159] and donors to such a fund possess only "advisory privileges" with respect to such expenditures and investments.[160] Moreover, as a matter of law the assets of a donor-advised fund belong to the public charity that holds the fund; they no longer belong to the donor.[161]

4.   Private Foundations: Regulated but Empowered Philanthropy

If an organization cannot qualify as a public charity under any of the three broad categories described in the preceding section, but if it still meets the overarching requirements applicable to Code section 501(c)(3) organizations, it will be classified as a private foundation.[162] Two broad subsets of private foundations are described in federal tax law.[163] While the most common is the non-operating or grant-making private foundation, tax law defines a much smaller group of private foundations. These foundations, which actually conduct charitable or other exempt programs – but due to their concentrated sources of financial support, do not qualify as public charities – often are referred to as private operating foundations.[164]

---

157   Such scrutiny is evidenced, for example, in a piece authored by two IRS agents who noted that a 1998 newspaper article painted a picture of the supporting organization form as "a kind of private foundation for the wealthy." Ron Shoemaker and Bill Brockner, *Public Charity Classification and Private Foundation Issues: Recent Emerging Significant Developments*, Continuing Professional Education Exempt Organizations Technical Instruction Program for Fiscal Year 2000 (Internal Revenue Service) 221, 222 (citing Monica Langley, *Gimme Shelter: The SO Trend: How to Succeed in Charity Without Really Giving*, WALL STREET JOURNAL (May 29, 1998) at A1).

158   *See* Hopkins and Blazek, *The Legal Answer Book for Private Foundations*, *supra* note 156, at p. 249.

159   *See* Code secs. 4966 and 4967.

160   *See* Code sec. 4966(d)(2)(A)(iii).

161   *See* Code sec. 4966(d)(2)(A)(ii).

162   *See* Code sec. 509(a).

163   There is no legal distinction or definition associated with the terms "family foundation" or "company foundation." These terms simply denote the source of a private foundation's assets. *See, e.g.,* Jerry J. McCoy and Kathryn W. Miree, *Family Foundation Handbook* (CCH, 2006) at p. 2-3 (describing the non-legal use of the term "family foundation").

164   *See* Code sec. 4942(j)(3). This book does not discuss in any length the rules governing private operating foundations and an even more narrowly described subset called "exempt operating foundations," which enjoy relief from the net investment income tax under Code section 4940(d)(2).

A proper understanding of the regulation of private non-operating foundations, which represent a primary source of grants to charities both domestically and
internationally, is critically important to a complete analysis of the laws impacting
philanthropic activity in the United States. The distinction between private foundations and public charities dates to the 1960s, when Congress responded to public concern over the perceived abuse of closely-held charities by holding high-profile
hearings and ultimately passing the Tax Reform Act of 1969.[165] The resulting web of
special rules uniquely applicable to private foundations reflects legislative concern for
the lack of built-in public accountability of such organizations relative to their public
charity counterparts, whose numerous donors and other stakeholders perform an
oversight function largely absent from the private foundation context. These complex
rules, often counterintuitive and widely feared by philanthropy professionals and legal
practitioners,[166] constitute the subject of multiple book-length treatises and hundreds
of pages of regulations. They can only be briefly summarized herein.

a.   The tax on net investment income

Despite their general exemption from federal income tax, most private foundations
actually do pay a limited income tax on the investment income they generate.[167] The
tax generally amounts to two percent of a foundation's annual net investment income,[168] and it may be reduced to one percent for any year in which a foundation's
payout for qualifying charitable expenditures exceeds its average of such payouts over
the preceding five years.[169]

b.   The minimum payout requirement

Perhaps the most well-known private foundation rule is the requirement to pay out a
minimum annual amount – essentially five percent of net asset value – for charitable
purposes.[170] To meet the statutory definition of a "qualifying distribution," which
counts toward the required payout amount, a private foundation's expenditure must
be paid both for an allowable purpose and to an allowable recipient. Allowable pur-

---

165   H.R. 13270, 91st Cong., Pub. L. 91-172 (1970). For a comprehensive overview of the political and social
      background of the legislative process leading to passage of this act, including the Treasury
      Department's study of and reports on alleged abuses by family-controlled foundations, see Waldemar
      A. Nielsen, *The Big Foundations* (Columbia University Press, 1972), at p. 8 (regarding Treasury reports)
      and pp. 3-20 (in general).

166   See Bruce R. Hopkins and Jody Blazek, *The Legal Answer Book for Private Foundations* (John Wiley & Sons,
      2002), at title page (leading off a practical guide for private foundations by noting the statement by a
      participant in one of Hopkins' seminars that "[t]he private foundation rules are really scary").

167   Exempt operating foundations are relieved from this tax obligation by Code sec. 4940(d).

168   Code sec. 4940(a).

169   See Code sec. 4940(e).

170   See generally Code sec. 4942 and the Treasury Regulations promulgated thereunder. The minimum
      mandatory payout technically is defined by calculating a foundation's "minimum investment return,"
      defined in Code section 4942(e), and modifying that calculation as provided in Code section 4942(d).

poses include the fundamental charitable, educational, religious, and other purposes identified in the federal deductibility rules.[171] Significantly, qualifying distributions also include "reasonable and necessary administrative expenses,"[172] thus including, for example, reasonable compensation paid to administrative employees and outside contractors.

The universe of allowable recipients of "qualifying distributions" can be delimited only by reference to multiple statutory and regulatory provisions. In general, a qualifying distribution includes an amount paid for permissible purposes to an individual, to a Code section 509(a)(1) or 509(a)(2) public charity, and to most supporting organizations described in Code section 509(a)(3).[173] Accordingly, a grant by a private foundation to another private non-operating foundation will not count toward the minimum payout requirement unless the grant is redistributed subject to strict accounting and documentation rules.[174]

If a foundation fails to meet its annual qualifying distribution requirement, it must pay an excise tax equivalent to 30 percent of its shortfall.[175] If the shortfall is not paid within the next tax year (in addition to that year's required minimum payout), an additional tax equivalent to 100 percent of the original shortfall will be levied.[176] Repeated failures to meet the payout requirement ultimately could lead to the revocation of private foundation status altogether.[177]

c.   *Taxable expenditures*

While private foundations are affirmatively required to make a certain amount of qualifying distributions to permissible recipients for charitable purposes, certain other types of payments constitute "taxable expenditures" under Code section 4945. A regime of prohibitively steep excise taxes essentially prohibits such expenditures altogether.[178]

---

171   *See* Code sec. 4942(g)(1)(A), referring to purposes defined in Code sec. 170(c)(2)(B).

172   *Id.*

173   *See id.,* which also carves out from the definition payments to otherwise allowable public charities that are controlled by the foundation or its disqualified persons. *See also* Code sec. 4942(g)(1)(B), which includes as qualifying distributions payments to acquire property used to accomplish the foundation's charitable purposes, and Code sec. 4942(g)(4)(A), which defines non-functionally integrated Type III supporting organizations, payments to which do not constitute "qualifying distributions" by private foundations.

174   *See* Code sec. 4942(g)(3).

175   *See* Code sec. 4942(a).

176   *See* Code sec. 4942(b).

177   *See* Code sec. 507(a)(2), which authorizes the IRS to terminate private foundation status for "willful repeated acts" or any "willful and flagrant act" leading to liability for one of the private foundation excise taxes.

178   *See* Code secs. 4945(a)(1) and (b)(1), which impose on the offending private foundation an initial tax equivalent to 20 percent of the taxable expenditure and, if the expenditure is not corrected within the prescribed period, a second-tier tax equivalent to 100 percent of the taxable expenditure. Foundation

Among the expenditures classified as taxable – and therefore essentially prohibited – for private foundations are any payments to engage in lobbying or political campaign activities.[179] While these provisions generally track the limitation on lobbying and the prohibition on politicking found in Code section 501(c)(3) for all charitable organizations, the outright bar[180] on lobbying is unique to private foundations and constitutes an important operational restraint for grant making foundations that support civil society programs and other public policy-related activity.[181]

Private foundations also may not make scholarship grants to individuals in the absence of an objective, non-discriminatory procedure approved in advance by the IRS, as such grants are classified as taxable expenditures.[182] To avoid running afoul of this rule, a private foundation may wish to include in its exemption application a request for the IRS to approve a scholarship procedure that is formulated to comport with the requirements outlined in federal regulations. A well-designed procedure will be broad enough to countenance virtually any scholarship to a student enrolled at a college or university as well as the funding of many creative projects outside formal educational institutional settings.

The list of taxable expenditures in the Internal Revenue Code also includes any other payments for purposes that are not charitable, educational, religious, or otherwise enumerated in the Code sections governing the deductibility of gifts by individuals.[183] Again, this prohibition generally tracks the operational restriction applicable to all organizations exempt under Code section 501(c)(3), i.e., that such organizations must be operated exclusively for charitable or other exempt purposes. As described earlier, however, the general operational test in Code section 501(c)(3) does not bar non-charitable activities and expenses that do not constitute more than an insubstan-

---

managers who authorize such expenditures willfully, without reasonable cause, and knowing that they constitute taxable expenditures may be personally subject to two tiers of taxes equivalent to 5 percent and 50 percent of the taxable expenditure, respectively, subject to a specified dollar cap. See Code secs. 4945(a)(2) and (b)(2). Moreover, willful repeated taxable expenditures, or even one willful and flagrant taxable expenditure, could jeopardize an offending organization's private foundation status. See Code sec. 507(a)(2).

179   Code sec. 4945(d)(1)-(2).

180   The effect of this taxable expenditure rule has correctly been described by one commentator as a "flat prohibition against 'political and propaganda activity'." Waldemar A. Nielsen, The Big Foundations (Columbia University Press, 1972), at p. 375.

181   See, e.g., Treas. Reg. sec. 53.4945-2(a)(5)-(6), which clarifies that grants to public charities may constitute taxable expenditures if they are "earmarked" for lobbying or inevitably will be used for lobbying (i.e., because the grantee's budget for the project funded by a grant does not contain sufficient non-lobbying expenses to ensure that the foundation's grant will not be used for lobbying).

182   Code secs. 4945(d)(3) and 4945(g). The restriction encompasses grants for "travel, study, or other similar purposes" and applies to scholarships that subsidize tuition and other allowable fees charged by colleges and universities as well as grants designed to assist individuals in developing skills outside an institutional setting (e.g., to produce musical or artistic works). See Code sec. 4945(g)(1) and (3).

183   See Code sec. 4945(d)(5), which addresses expenditures for purposes other than those described in Code section 170(c)(2)(B).

tial portion of an organization's aggregate activities and expenses.[184] Private founda-tions, by contrast, may not incur expenses for *any* non-charitable activities.

Finally, and perhaps most importantly for a consideration of legal constraints on philanthropy (both domestically and internationally), taxable expenditures include grants to certain categories of organizations, including most private foundations, a few public charities, and any organization not described in Code section 501(c)(3), unless the foundation also complies with a list of pre- and post-grant due diligence require-ments known as "expenditure responsibility."[185] As a practical matter, this provision precludes most non-public charities – including private foundations – from obtaining grants from private foundations. Indeed, many private foundations categorically decline grant requests that would require them to follow the onerous and complex requirements of expenditure responsibility.

The expenditure responsibility rules are examined in greater detail in Chapter Three's discussion of private foundation grants to foreign organizations. In general, the rules are designed to require private foundations to ensure that grants are used for their intended charitable purpose, obtain sufficient documentation of expenses from recipients, and make adequate reports to the IRS regarding the use of such grants.[186]

For private foundations desiring to avoid expenditure responsibility, grants must be made only to permissible public charities, a group that includes the functio-nally based categories of public charities and the broadly publicly supported public charities described earlier in sections III(3)(a) and III(3)(b) of this chapter. Grants to supporting organizations, described in section III(3)(c), also are permitted without expenditure responsibility unless (i) a supporting organization is a non-functionally integrated "Type III" organization or (ii) a disqualified person of the grantor foundation controls either the supporting organization seeking the grant or one or more of the public charities supported by the supporting organization.[187]

In light of these taxable expenditure rules, a organization seeking a grant from a private foundation usually (that is, if the foundation is well-administered) will be re-quired to submit evidence of its public charity classification and, if it is a supporting organization, documentation to allow the foundation to determine whether the sup-porting organization is a non-functionally integrated "Type III" organization. (The pri-vate foundation itself should be able to determine whether its disqualified persons exercise impermissible control over the grantee or its supported organizations.) These evidentiary requirements increase the time and expense required for private foun-

---

184   *See* discussion *supra* at section III(1)(B) of Chapter Two.
185   *See* Code sec. 4945(d)(4). Grants may be made to exempt operating foundations without exercising expenditure responsibility. *See* Code sec. 4945(d)(4)(A)(iii).
186   *See* Code sec. 4945(h) and the Treasury Regulations promulgated thereunder.
187   *See* Code secs. 4945(d)(4)(A)(ii) and 4942(g)(4)(A).

dations to conduct philanthropic activity. They also may effectively weed out some smaller and/or less sophisticated grant seekers who do not understand the taxable expenditure rules and therefore may inaccurately perceive documentation requirements imposed by private foundations as arbitrary or otherwise designed to discourage them from applying.

d.   The prohibition on self-dealing

Pursuant to the punitively high excise taxes imposed by Code section 4941(a) and (b), a private foundation generally may not engage in any financial transactions with certain insiders of the foundation, described in federal tax law as "disqualified persons"[188] and generally including the foundation's officers, directors, trustees, "substantial contributors" (generally including any person who contributes more than two percent of the total lifetime-to-date contributions received by the foundation by the end of any tax year),[189] and certain related family members and business entities.[190] Such prohibited "self-dealing" between a foundation and its disqualified persons encompasses virtually any provision of goods, other property, or services, whether by sale, lease, loan, or other means of transfer.[191] Limited exceptions permit certain transactions between private foundations and disqualified persons, including the payment of compensation by a foundation to a disqualified person for "personal services" rendered to the foundation that are "reasonable and necessary" to carrying out the foundation's charitable purposes,[192] the making of an interest-free loan by a disqualified person to a private foundation for charitable purposes,[193] and the rent-free lease of property by a disqualified person to a foundation.[194]

The self-dealing bar is totally prohibitive: it does not countenance arms' length, fair market value transactions between private foundations and their disqualified persons (subject to the limited exceptions noted above).[195] The bar also carries severe financial consequences: the self-dealer (i.e., the disqualified person) is subject to a tax in the amount of ten percent of the transaction's value,[196] and any foundation officer

---

188   See generally Code sec. 4941.

189   See Code sec. 507(d)(2).

190   See generally Code sec. 4946.

191   Code sec. 4941(d)(1).

192   See Code sec. 4941(d)(2)(E). The regulations indicate that such services include legal services, investment counseling, and banking. See Treas. Reg. sec. 53.4941(d)-3(c).

193   See Code sec. 4941(d)(2)(B).

194   See Code sec. 4941(d)(2)(C).

195   Public charities, by contrast, may engage in transactions with their disqualified persons (a group of natural and legal persons defined slightly differently than in the private foundation context) on terms that do not confer an "excess benefit" to the disqualified person in question. See generally Code sec. 4958 and the Treasury Regulations promulgated thereunder.

196   Code sec. 4941(a)(1). An additional tax, equivalent to 200 percent of the transaction's value, is imposed on the self-dealer if the transaction is not unwound within a statutory period. Code sec. 4941(b)(1).

or director who authorizes a self-dealing transaction willfully and without reasonable cause, knowing that it constitutes self-dealing, may be subject to a tax equal to five percent of the transaction value, subject to a dollar cap.[197] Moreover, a private foundation that willfully engages in repeated self-dealing transactions – or even one such willful and flagrant transaction – could jeopardize its private foundation status.[198]

e.   *The excess business holdings prohibition*

Private foundations may invest in business enterprises for the purpose of generating income that supports their charitable grant making and operations. Nevertheless, such investment activity is circumscribed in ways that do not similarly bind public charities. One of two significant restrictions effectively precludes private foundations from owning more than a certain percentage of the interest in any business enterprise by imposing a prohibitively steep excise tax on such "excess business holdings."[199]

Under these rules, the ceiling on ownership by private foundations generally is fixed at 20 percent of an enterprise's total ownership interest, *e.g.*, voting stock in a corporation or profits interests in a partnership.[200] Importantly, holdings of a foundation's disqualified persons generally must be aggregated with the foundation's direct holdings in determining whether the 20 percent ceiling has been exceeded.[201] Foundations that receive gifts of business holdings generally have five years to dispose of such holdings without violating the excess business holdings prohibition.[202]

By limiting the extent of private foundation ownership in business enterprises, the excess business holdings rule restrains the voice and control of private foundations in the affairs of commercial ventures. The rule clearly affects closely held corporations and partnerships by preventing the use of private foundations as a tool for control of such enterprises. In addition, however, the rule impacts publicly traded companies by

---

197   Code secs. 4941(a)(2) (establishing the applicability of such taxes to "foundation managers") and 4946(b) (defining "foundation manager" to include officers and directors). If the transaction is not unwound within the time prescribed by statute, an additional tax may be levied on an officer or director in an amount equal to 50 percent of the transaction's value, subject to a maximum penalty. Code sec. 4941(b)(2).

198   *See* Code sec. 507(a)(2).

199   *See* Code sec. 4943(a)-(b), in which two tiers of tax are imposed on the private foundation: 10 percent of the excess business holdings at the first tier, and an additional 200 percent tax on such holdings that are not disposed of within a specified period. Repeated willful violations of the excess business holdings rule, or one such willful and flagrant violation, also could jeopardize an organization's private foundation status altogether. *See* Code sec. 507(a)(2).

200   Code sec. 4943(c)(2) and (3). With the 20 percent ownership ceiling, a private foundation by definition may not own a sole proprietorship. Code sec. 4943(c)(3)(B).

201   Code sec. 4943(c)(2)(A)(ii). Nevertheless, if a foundation does not directly own more than a two percent direct stake in a corporation (measured in this case by either vote or value), it will not be deemed as owning excess business holdings, regardless of the extent of its disqualified persons' holdings. *See* Code sec. 4943(c)(2)(C).

202   *See* Code sec. 4943(c)(6).

restricting excessive ownership in such companies by private foundations – including foundations created and controlled by such companies, which otherwise conceivably could be used by companies to prevent takeovers and otherwise block actions on behalf of other shareholders.

f.   The prohibition on jeopardy investments

Another restriction unique to private foundations is the bar on so-called "jeopardy investments." Pursuant to this rule in Code section 4944, private foundations are subject to tax – once again at a confiscatory level – on any investments that jeopardize the foundation's ability to undertake its charitable or other exempt purposes.[203]

But what exactly is a "jeopardy investment"? The Treasury Regulations provide that no particular investments categorically will be deemed to jeopardize a private foundation's exempt purposes, instead adopting a case-by-case approach that takes into account the foundation's entire program of investments.[204] Nevertheless, certain types of investments are subject to higher levels of scrutiny, including margin trading of securities, commodity futures, and short sales.[205] The relevant analysis focuses on whether a private foundation's directors, officers, or trustees exercise "ordinary business care and prudence" in investing so that the foundation is not precluded from continuing its charitable operations in both the short and long term.[206]

Several important exceptions apply to the jeopardy investment rules. Investments donated to a private foundation are not subject to the excise tax under Code section 4944.[207] Additionally, investments acquired as part of certain corporate reorganizations are exempt from the tax.[208] Finally, if the primary purpose of an investment is to accomplish one or more charitable, educational, or other exempt purposes, and no significant purpose of the investment is to produce income or effect the appreciation of property, the investment is not subject to the Code section tax.[209] Such

---

203   See Code secs. 4944(a)(1) and 4944(b)(1), which levy an initial ten percent tax on any such "jeopardy investment" and an additional 25 percent tax if the investment is not unwound within the prescribed period. Similarly, Code section 4944(a)(2) imposes a ten percent tax on foundation managers who knowingly make jeopardy investments on behalf of a private foundation willfully and without reasonable cause, and Code section 4944(b)(2) imposes an additional five percent tax on such managers who refuse to agree to unwind a jeopardy investment within the statutory time period, but subject to maximum dollar caps. Code section 507(a)(2) places an organization's private foundation status at risk for willful repeated jeopardy investments or even one willful and flagrant jeopardy investment.

204   Treas. Reg. sec. 53.4944-1(a)(2).

205   Id.

206   See id.

207   Treas. Reg. sec. 53.4944-1(a)(2)(ii)(a).

208   Treas. Reg. sec. 53.4944-1(a)(2)(ii)(b).

209   See Code sec. 4944(c); see also Treas. Reg. sec. 53.4944-3. Notably, Treas. Reg. section 53.4944-3(a)(1)(iii) prohibits lobbying or political campaign activity as a purpose of such investments. Such expenditures arguably also would result in taxable expenditures under Code sections 4945(d)(1)-(2) and (5).

"program-related investments" or "PRIs" represent alternative avenues to achieving charitable or other exempt objectives,[210] and they will be revisited in Chapter Three's discussion of current developments in the regulation of international philanthropy by private foundations.

g.   Additional private foundation rules

The foregoing summary of rules and restrictions, while by no means designed to comprise an exhaustive list, illustrates the special burdens associated with classification as a private foundation. Two additional features underscore the relative disadvantages of life as a private foundation rather than a public charity: the scope of the annual return filing requirement and the public nature of donor information contained in such returns.

Private foundations, like public charities, are obligated to file annual federal returns. Form 990-PF is the return prescribed by the IRS specifically for private foundations.[211] Unlike public charities, however, private foundations are obligated to file this return regardless of income level; there is no exception for "small" foundations.[212] This universal reporting requirement for private foundations can create a significant burden on foundations with limited resources, and it should be carefully considered, along with other administrative and compliance-related requirements, when analyzing whether a private foundation represents the most effective and efficient vehicle for accomplishing the philanthropic goals of an individual, family, or company.[213]

The three most recent annual returns filed by public charities (Form 990) and private foundations (Form 990-PF) are subject to public inspection.[214] As noted earlier, however, while public charities may redact information when publishing such returns that otherwise would identify donors to their organizations, private foundations may not make such redactions.[215] As a result, substantial contributors to private foundations, and the amounts of their contributions, are readily identifiable by examining the publicly available returns of private foundations at www.guidestar.org or other sources.[216] This publicity simply comes with the territory when establishing a private

---

210   *See* Donald McGee Etheridge, Jr., "Private Foundations – Section 4940 and Section 4944," 468 Tax Mgmt. (BNA) Estates, Gifts, and Trusts, A-1 (2011), at p. A-22 ("Section 4944(c) represents congressional recognition and approval of the fact that foundations often carry out their exempt activities through methods other than direct grants").

211   *See supra* note 94 and accompanying text.

212   *See* Code sec. 6033(a)(3)(A)(ii).

213   As discussed in section III(3)(c) of this chapter, donor-advised funds, embedded within public charities, represent a popular alternative.

214   *See* Code sec. 6104(b) and (d)(2) and Treas. Reg. sec. 301.6104(d)-1(b)(4)(iii); *see also* discussion in section III(2)(c) of this chapter.

215   *See* Code sec. 6104(b) and section III(2)(c) of this chapter.

216   This information must be provided in Schedule B to Form 990-PF.

foundation. While it may deter some would-be philanthropists from utilizing the private foundation form, it also represents one of the many channels utilized in tax-exempt law to regulate closely held charities by subjecting them to rigorous public scrutiny.

5.   Deductibility of Charitable Gifts by Individuals and Corporations

Private foundations represent a significant portion of the philanthropic sector, and a proper understanding of the laws governing private foundations therefore constitutes a critical component in analyzing how the American legal system generally affects philanthropic activity. For many Americans, however, private foundations are more ideal than real; they may be perceived as philanthropic vehicles available only to the rich while out of reach to individuals, families, and businesses with charitable impulses but more modest means. Even where wealth is not a bar to the creation of a private foundation, some individual and institutional donors may not want to create separate legal entities as vehicles for their charity, preferring instead to give directly to organizations that carry out charitable, educational, religious, and other "exempt" activities.

For the vast majority of Americans, philanthropy is defined by direct charitable giving. And for many of them, the most significant laws affecting philanthropy are found in the federal income tax rules governing the deductibility of charitable gifts. Pursuant to these rules, individuals who itemize their deductions, along with corporations, may be able to deduct their qualifying contributions to charitable organizations from their adjusted gross income when calculating liability for federal income tax. Generally speaking (and subject to overall caps and other limitations, as discussed below), one's income tax liability will be reduced by the percentage of a charitable gift that corresponds to the taxpayer's marginal tax rate. For an individual who is subject to income tax at the current maximum federal rate of 39.6 percent, therefore, each dollar of a charitable gift will reduce his or her tax liability by 39.6 cents. Indeed, the tax advantage conferred by the charitable contribution deduction represents perhaps the most important American legal tool available to promote American philanthropy. As such, the rules governing deductibility for charitable gifts warrant a broad discussion herein.

a.   Introduction to the deductibility rules

Under current tax law rules,[217] certain charitable contributions may be deducted from the taxable income of both individuals and corporations.[218] Specifically, federal tax law provides deductibility for "contribution[s] or gift[s] to or for the use of" specified governmental units and other organizations.[219] Among the most prominent organizations identified by statute are those organized and operated exclusively for charitable, educational, and other purposes described in Code section 501(c)(3).[220]

Not every payment to an eligible organization, of course, is eligible for deduction as a "contribution or gift." Individuals and corporations make many other types of payments to charitable, educational, and religious organizations, including tuition payments to schools; purchases of performance tickets from symphonies, orchestras, and theaters; and purchases of books and other items from churches, schools, and other organizations that are tax-exempt under Code section 501(c)(3). The *sine qua non* of a deductible contribution or gift is that it must be, in fact, a gift: in the language of a famous passage from a 1960 decision of the United States Supreme Court, the payment must be made out of a "detached or disinterested generosity."[221] Payments made in exchange for goods or services, *e.g.*, tuition payments for the receipt of educational services, or payments for the purchase of performance tickets, do not flow from the "generosity" of the payor. On the contrary, they represent consideration in exchange for value received, and therefore such payments do not constitute deductible contributions or gifts.[222]

Deductible contributions to or for the benefit of charitable organizations include only contributions of money or property. Contributions of in-kind services to a

---

217   As discussed below, various reform proposals continue to receive scrutiny by members of Congress, the Obama administration, and others in the context of ongoing discussions regarding the reduction of federal budget deficits and simplification of the federal income tax regime. As discussed in section III(5)(e) of this chapter, many of these proposals could affect the extent to which charitable gifts would continue to be deductible for federal income tax purposes.

218   *See* Code sec. 170(a). While beyond the scope of this paper, charitable contributions by an *estate* also may be deducted from the gross income of the estate for purposes of the federal estate tax rules, and such contributions also may be deductible when computing federal *gift* tax. *See* Code secs. 2055(a)(2) (estate tax) and 2522(a)(2) (gift tax).

219   *See* Code sec. 170(c).

220   *See* Code sec. 170(c)(2)(B). To be eligible to receive deductible charitable contributions, an organization also must comply with the private inurement, lobbying, and political campaign activity restrictions in Code section 501(c)(3). *See* Code sec. 170(c)(2)(C)-(D).

221   *Commissioner v. Duberstein*, 363 U.S. 278, 285 (1960) (quoting *Commissioner v. LoBue*, 351 U.S. 243, 246 (1956)). Such generosity, in turn, must be measured by an "objective inquiry" into whether a gift has, in fact, been made. *Id.* at 286.

222   For purposes of the deductibility rules, "intangible religious benefits," such as participation in church services, are deemed to have no pecuniary value and thus do not preclude or reduce a donor's eligibility to deduct a gift or contribution (*e.g.*, a tithe or offering contribution) to a religious organization. *See* Code sec. 170(f)(8)(B)(iii) (providing that such benefits may be described in a written acknowledgment from the recipient organization without a quantification of value).

charitable organization, such as the pro bono provision of legal services to an animal shelter by a lawyer who serves on the shelter's governing board, are not deductible.[223]

One additional general limitation on deductibility warrants brief mention here but a fuller exposition in the examinations of international philanthropy in Chapters Three and Six. In general, individuals and corporations may not deduct gifts made to charitable organizations that are not formed in the United States or under United States law.[224] Moreover, corporations may not deduct charitable gifts to unincorporated domestic charitable organizations if such gifts will be used outside the United States or its possessions.[225]

b.   The documentation requirements associated with deductibility

For contributions of money and property to charitable organizations, proper documentation is a prerequisite to deductibility. As an initial matter, monetary gifts may not be deducted from gross income unless the donor maintains a bank record evidencing the gift or a written instrument from the recipient that documents the recipient's name and the date and amount of the gift.[226]

For monetary gifts of $250 or more, the documentation requirements are more detailed. To be eligible to deduct such a gift, a donor must obtain a "contemporaneous written acknowledgment" from the recipient that evidences the amount of the contribution (including a description of any noncash property contributed) and the value of any goods or services received in return by the donor, or, if no such return goods or services were received, then a statement to that effect.[227] In this context, a written acknowledgment is considered "contemporaneous" if the donor obtains it from the recipient by the date on which the donor files the annual return that reflects the deduction, or by the due date (with extensions) for such return, whichever is earlier.[228] The documentation requirements are strictly interpreted; if, for instance, the written acknowledgment from the recipient organization lacks any reference to whether

---

223   *See* Treas. Reg. sec. 1.170A-1(g). Nevertheless, unreimbursed "out-of-pocket" expenses may be deductible if they are incurred for the sole purpose of providing such *gratis* services to a charitable organizations. *See id.* Under this rule, the unreimbursed cost of wood and nails purchased by an unpaid volunteer who helps build a storage shed for a charitable youth camp could be deducted as a charitable contribution by the volunteer made "for the benefit" of the youth camp.

224   *See* Code sec. 170(c)(2)(A).

225   *See* Code sec. 170(c)(2) ("flush-left," non-indented text, which encompasses "trust[s], chest[s], fund[s], [and] foundation[s]"). Accordingly, qualifying gifts by corporations to United States charitable *corporations* may be eligible for deduction even though they may be used outside the United States. For further discussion on this issue, see Chapter Three.

226   Code sec. 170(f)(17).

227   Code sec. 170(f)(8)(A)-(B).

228   Code sec. 170(f)(8)(C).

goods or services were received in return by the donor, the deduction may be dis-allowed.[229]

The documentation requirements associated with the deductibility of *noncash* gifts of property are the most demanding of all. Although noncash gifts may not be the first type of giving that comes to mind for most people, they represent a sizable slice of American philanthropy. In 2008, for example, 23 million individuals reported $40.4 billion in itemized deductions associated with charitable contributions of non-cash property, $12.3 billion of which reflected gifts of corporate stock, and $7.9 billion of which reflected gifts of clothing.[230]

In view of the scope of noncash charitable giving, legislators and regulators have implemented stringent validation and quantification conditions for the deducti-bility of such gifts. These documentation requirements are progressively more onerous as the purported value of the gift increases. Under the current rules, in order to deduct a noncash gift of less than $250, a donor generally must maintain a written acknow-ledgment from the charitable recipient evidencing the donee's name and address, the date of the gift, and a detailed description of the donated property (with special rules for donated securities).[231] For noncash gifts of $250 to $500, a donor seeking deducti-bility must obtain a contemporaneous written acknowledgment meeting the require-ments for cash gifts of $250 or more.[232] For noncash gifts above $500 but not more than $5,000, deductibility requires not only the aforementioned contemporaneous written acknowledgment but also the completion and filing of IRS Form 8283, which requests detailed information about the property and the manner in which it was acquired.[233] Above $5,000 but at or below $500,000, deductibility for noncash gifts requires the contemporaneous written acknowledgment, Form 8283, and a qualified appraisal reflecting information required in the Treasury Regulations.[234] Finally, for noncash gifts of more than $500,000, the donor generally must meet all of the fore-going documentation requirements and attach the qualified appraisal to the return that reflects the claimed deduction.[235]

The documentation requirements associated with the deduction of charitable gifts of money and property represent an excellent example of the highly developed state of the legal regime to regulate charitable giving and curb abuse by those who

---

229   See, e.g., *Durden v. Commissioner*, T.C. Memo. 2012-140 (May 17, 2012).

230   Bruce R. Hopkins, *The Tax Law of Charitable Giving*, 4th ed. (John Wiley & Sons, 2010), 2012 Cumulative Supplement at p. 64, n. 68.1 (citing IRS, 30 *Statistics of Income Bulletin* (no. 3) 76 (2011)).

231   Proposed Treas. Reg. sec. 1.170A-16(a)(1).

232   Proposed Treas. Reg. sec. 1.170A-16(b); *see also* the preceding discussion of cash gift substantiation requirements.

233   Code sec. 170(f)(11)(B); Proposed Treas. Reg. sec. 1.170A-16(c).

234   Code sec. 170(f)(11)(C) and (E); Proposed Treas. Reg. secs. 1.170A-16(d) and 1.170A-17.

235   Code sec. 170(f)(11)(D); Proposed Treas. Reg. 1.170A-16(e).

seek to take undue advantage of the incentives to philanthropy offered by federal tax law. The rules are not airtight, but they provide an incredibly well delineated framework designed to minimize deduction fraud. As with any effective regulatory system, however, the documentation rules do impose administrative burdens on donors and recipient organizations alike. With respect to high-value gifts of noncash property, the rules may in fact discourage would-be donors from making such contributions in light of the extensive documentation and appraisal requirements.

c.   *The percentage limits on deductibility for charitable gifts by individuals and corporations*

The income tax deduction for charitable contributions is not unlimited. For corporations, the "cap" is established at ten percent of annual taxable income.[236] Corporate contributions of money and noncash property thus are deductible only to the extent they do not exceed ten percent of the corporate donor's taxable income for the year.[237] Excess charitable contributions, *i.e.*, contributions that are nondeductible in a particular tax year because they exceed the ten percent cap, generally may be carried forward and deducted in one of the five succeeding tax years, subject to specific annual limitations in the succeeding tax years.[238]

For individuals, the "cap" rules are somewhat more complicated. As an initial matter, more favorable caps apply in connection with gifts made to public charities rather than private foundations.[239] Monetary charitable contributions by an individual to public charities are deductible up to *50 percent* of the individual's adjusted gross income within a taxable year.[240] By contrast, individual monetary charitable contributions to private foundations may be deducted only to the extent they do not exceed *30 percent* of the individual's adjusted gross income within a taxable year.[241]

Charitable gifts of noncash property by individuals are subject to lower and more variable deductibility limits. For gifts of appreciated or "capital gain" property made by an individual to a public charity, such gifts generally may be deducted to the extent they do not exceed *30 percent* of the individual's adjusted gross income for the

---

236   Code sec. 170(b)(2)(A).

237   "Taxable income" in this statutory context is defined to include the adjusted amounts as specified in Treas. Reg. sec. 1.170A-11(a).

238   *See* Code sec. 170(d)(2)(A).

239   *See* section III(3)(c) of this chapter for a discussion of the extensive legal framework distinguishing the various classifications of public charities from the "default" private foundation classification under Code section 509(a).

240   *See* Code sec. 170(b)(1)(A), which provides for such deductibility up to 50 percent of an individual's "contribution base," and Code sec. 170(b)(1)(G), which defines "contribution base" as the individual's adjusted gross income with adjustments for net operating loss carrybacks.

241   *See* Code sec. 170(b)(1)(B).

taxable year.[242] With respect to individual gifts of capital gain property to a private foundation, such gifts are subject to a general deductibility limit of *20 percent* of the individual's adjusted gross income for the taxable year.[243]

As with charitable gifts by corporations, charitable contributions by individuals that have been capped by the applicable percentage limits on deductibility generally may be carried forward and deducted for up to five years. Such carried-forward deductions may be taken only to the extent that deductions for the then-current tax year do not equal or exceed that year's deductibility caps.[244]

d.   *Valuation rules for contributions of property*

In addition to the rules governing the substantiation of noncash gifts made to charities, similar special rules apply to the valuation of noncash property gifted to charity, whether by individual or corporate donors. While contributions of long-term capital gain property, *i.e.*, appreciated property, generally are deductible to the extent of the fair market value of the property, most contributions of ordinary income and short-term capital gain property, *e.g.*, inventory, are deductible only to the extent of the donor's adjusted basis in the property.[245] One significant exception exists, however, to this limitation-of-basis rule for gifts of inventory: if the inventory is donated to a public charity and used by the public charity "solely for the care of the ill, the needy, or infants" and meets certain other statutory and regulatory requirements, *e.g.*, regarding documentation by the recipient, the gift may be eligible for enhanced deductibility above the normal basis limitation.[246]

e.   *Current proposals to limit deductibility*

As of February 2013, the United States federal government faces an arguably unprecedented combination of systemic fiscal challenges, including an accumulated debt of over $16 trillion;[247] entrenched programs of expenditures in Social Security, Medicare and Medicaid, national defense, and other areas, which cannot easily be reduced by legislators who fear their re-election efforts would be sabotaged by supporting such

---

242   *See* Code sec. 170(b)(1)(C)(i).

243   *See* Code sec. 170(b)(1)(D)(i)(I).

244   For the carry-forward rules applicable to the various individual deductibility limits, *see* Code secs. 170(d)(1) (monetary gifts to public charities), 170(b)(1)(B) ("flush-left," non-indented text; monetary gifts to private foundations), 170(b)(1)(C)(ii) (gifts of capital gain property to public charities), and 170(b)(1)(D)(ii) (gifts of capital gain property to private foundations).

245   *See* Code sec. 170(e)(1).

246   *See* Code sec. 170(e)(3). For a helpful summary of the enhanced deductibility for qualified gifts of inventory, *see* Victoria B. Bjorklund and Joanna Pressman, "Cross-Border Philanthropy," in Penina Kessler Lieber and Donald R. Levy, eds., *Complete Guide to Nonprofit Organizations* (Civic Research Institute, 2005), at pp. 10-11 and 10-12.

247   *See* the "U.S. National Debt Clock" at http://www.brillig.com/debt_clock/ (web site last visited on March 3, 2013).

reductions; and historically low federal income tax rates engineered by tax cuts implemented in 2001, which originally were due to expire in 2010 but were extended through the end of 2012 and then eliminated only for those with taxable income exceeding $400,000 ($450,000 for married couples filing jointly).

In an election year, any tax increase would constitute a politically problematic notion. Nevertheless, the "perfect storm" of national budgetary challenges forced Congress and the Obama administration to discuss an array of proposals to reduce the deficit. Predictably, however such discussions did not produce any agreed-upon changes until after the election – and even then, such changes only encompassed tax hikes on the wealthiest Americans, but not changes to deductions. As of early 2013, however, deductibility changes remain very much a focus of lawmakers' proposals for deficit reduction. Among the areas under discussion is the deduction for charitable gifts and contributions.

The notion that the long-standing deduction for charitable contributions could be limited or eliminated causes consternation for many, and not simply because Americans have grown accustomed to the deduction since its introduction in the early twentieth century. Conceptually, the deduction has been justified on the grounds that charitable donations do not affect the stream of commerce as do the consumption of goods and services or the creation of wealth, both of which are subject to taxation.[248] Nevertheless, at least for some policymakers, the federal government's current fiscal dilemma has rendered the charitable deduction fair game.

In his proposed budget for the 2013 fiscal year, President Obama initially suggested limiting the extent of the charitable deduction for relatively high-income taxpayers, defined as incomes exceeding $200,000 for individuals and $250,000 for married couples.[249] The president's proposal would have limited the reduction in tax associated with the deduction to a maximum of 28 percent, even if the taxpayer's marginal tax rate exceeds 28 percent. Under this approach, a married couple with taxable income of $500,000 and charitable contributions of $50,000 would have seen their deduction associated with those contributions shrink from $17,500 (based on the top 2012 tax rate of 35 percent) to $14,000.[250]

---

248   See *Sweetened Charity*, THE ECONOMIST, June 9, 2012, at 29. Former Secretary of Labor Robert Reich, however, notes that charitable donations reflect a unique type of personal consumption, *viz.*, a choice regarding the utilization of one's personal resources. *Id.* at pp. 29-30.

249   See Lisa Chiu, *Nonprofits Oppose Obama Plan on Limiting Charity Write-Offs*, THE CHRONICLE OF PHILANTHROPY/PHILANTHROPY TODAY (Feb. 13, 2012), http://philanthropy.com/article/Nonprofits-Oppose-Obama-Plan/130776/.

250   Under the new top tax rate of 39.6 percent, the value of this married couple's deduction would have been reduced even more, from $19,800 to $14,000. For a different policy perspective, which advises maintaining the tax favored treatment of charitable contributions by high-income individuals particularly if tax rates on such individuals are increased, *see* Robert J. Shiller, *Taxes Needn't Discourage Philanthropy*, NEW YORK TIMES (July 28, 2012) (http://www.nytimes.com/2012/07/29/business/if-raising-top-tax-rates-encourage-charitable-giving.html?_r=0).

Congressional Republicans serving on the Joint Select Committee on Deficit Reduction proposed a different approach to deductibility limits as a means of trimming the national deficit. This proposal would have affected not only charitable contributions but all other "itemized" deductions, i.e., deductible expenses listed on Schedule A of IRS Form 1040, including not only charitable contributions but also real estate and sales taxes, mortgage interest, and others. Under the Republicans' plan, all such itemized deductions in the aggregate would have been capped at two percent of a taxpayer's adjusted gross income.[251] The authors of the academic paper on which the congressional plan was based estimated that under this new approach, three-quarters of taxpayers who currently itemize their deductions instead would have elected to take the standard deduction.[252]

Such proposals by the administration and Congress could significantly dampen charitable giving, as studies suggest a direct correlation between the availability of deductions and levels of private philanthropy.[253] In addition, other factors could significantly reduce utility of the charitable contribution deduction to individual taxpayers. For instance, some proposals would reduce marginal tax rates but increase overall income subject to tax by closing so-called "loopholes." The presidentially appointed National Commission on Fiscal Responsibility and Reform (the "Simpson-Bowles Commission") suggested such an approach, which potentially would lower the value of the deduction for taxpayers in all brackets.[254]

Finally, exacerbating all new policy proposals that would cap deductibility is the reinstatement of the rule that formerly reduced itemized deductions for taxpayers by three percent of the amount by which adjusted gross income exceeded a prescribed ceiling. This reduction rule was phased out temporarily from 2006-2010 as part of President George W. Bush's tax cuts implemented in 2001, but the phase-out was extended for 2011 and 2012 as part of tax legislation adopted in late 2010.[255]

Any of the above-described legislative proposals (the reinstatement of the "reduction rule" is more than a proposal; it took effect in 2013 in the absence of any

---

251   Suzanne Perry, *Charitable Deduction Faces a Fresh Challenge as Lawmakers Attempt to Close Deficit*, THE
        CHRONICLE OF PHILANTHROPY/TAX WATCH (Nov. 17, 2011), http://philanthropy.com/article/Charitable-
        Deduction-Faces-a/129815/.

252   *Id.*

253   *See, e.g.,* Center on Philanthropy at Indiana University, *The 2010 Study of High Net Worth Philanthropy*
        (2010), available at http://www.philanthropy.iupui.edu/research-by-category/the-2010-study-of-high-
        net-worth-philanthropy, which notes at page 47 that two-thirds of wealthy Americans report their
        giving would "somewhat" or "dramatically" decrease in the absence of the deduction for charitable
        contributions.

254   *See* Laura Saunders, *Charitable Deductions Under Fire*, WALL STREET JOURNAL (June 8, 2012). For example,
        if an individual currently in the 28 percent bracket saw his or her rate reduced to 25 percent, his or her
        charitable contribution deduction would be three percent less valuable.

255   Diane Freda, *Pease Amendment on Itemized Deductions Alive and Well and Scheduled for 2013*, BLOOMBERG
        BNA DAILY TAX REPORT, May 29, 2012.

congressional action to extend relief from the rule) could significantly discourage philanthropic giving in the United States by reducing the value of the federal income tax deduction associated with charitable gifts and contributions. Predictably, nonprofit sector professionals fear that their organizations stand to lose significant income if any of the proposals is adopted, and many have voiced their concern.[256] As of late February 2013, their efforts appear to be bearing fruit: following extensive hearings in the House Ways and Means Committee regarding the charitable deduction, Senate Democrats spared only the charitable contribution deduction from the proposed elimination of all credits and deductions for annual taxpayers with annual income exceeding $1 million.[257]

Alarmed nonprofit professionals in the United States might take heart by looking to the United Kingdom, which offers an interesting comparative study in contemporary deductibility reform efforts – and the political pressure faced by those who propose such reforms. When the highest marginal income tax rate in the UK recently was reduced from 50 to 45 percent (still higher than the recently-increased top US rate of 39.6 percent), Chancellor of the Exchequer George Osborne also originally announced the imposition of a first-ever cap on the deductibility of charitable contributions, which would have limited deductions to 25 percent of income above £50,000 (approximately $80,000).[258] That plan, however, was abandoned after charities voiced their displeasure to the British government, which subsequently suggested a compromise capping deductions at perhaps 50 percent of a taxpayer's total income (similar to the limit under United States law for contributions to public charities).[259]

Chancellor Osborne's experience may provide encouragement for charities in the United States, where the charitable contribution deduction arguably constitutes an even more entrenched feature of the social and fiscal landscape than in the United Kingdom. In short, caps on the deductibility of charitable gifts could affect philanthropy negatively by devaluing the tax incentives currently associated with such gifts; but deductibility caps seem unlikely to be adopted in the United States without a fight, even in the current gloomy fiscal climate.

---

256   See. e.g., Chiu, *supra* note 249 (quoting a critique of President Obama's proposed 28 percent cap by Diana Aviv, CEO of Independent Sector).

257   See Alliance for Charitable Reform, "An Active Week in Washington on the Charitable Deduction" (Anne Urban, "Consider This ..." Blog), Feb. 22, 2013, http://acreform.com/blog/an_active_week_in_washington_on_the_charitable_deduction/ (web site last visited on March 3, 2013).

258   *See One Hand Giveth*, The Economist, April 21, 2012, p. 72.

259   Alliance for Charitable Reform, "U.K. Abandons Plan to Curb Tax Incentives," June 1, 2012, http://acreform.com/blog/u.k._considers plan_to_limit_charitable_giving_incentive/ (web site last visited on March 3, 2013).

Chapter Three:

United States Legal Frameworks Affecting
International Philanthropic Giving

Chapter Two, notwithstanding its length, offers only a summary of the vast, multi-layered system of laws that generally affect philanthropic activity in the United States. Throughout the discussions of federal and state tax exemptions for charitable organi-zations, the organizational and operational rules governing tax-exempt charities, the special rules affecting private foundations, general reporting and disclosure obliga-tions, the deductibility of charitable gifts and contributions, and other areas, a com-mon theme emerges: philanthropy in the United States is both encouraged and tightly regulated by a robust, mature framework of laws governing charities themselves and those who support them. Obvious incentives, such as exemption itself and the ability of donors to reduce their tax burden by giving to exempt organizations, are balanced by a dizzying array of restrictions and limitations that effectively curb fraud by donors as well as abuse and waste by charities.

American philanthropy, however, does not stop at national borders. Individuals, corporations, and private foundations support charitable work conducted throughout the world by American organizations and, to a far lesser degree, by foreign organiza-tions. Chapter Three reviews the most important United States laws governing philan-thropic support for international charitable efforts, including deductibility restrictions, rules governing grants by private foundations, and giving to United States charities that conduct or support foreign charitable programs.[260]

As the rules explained in this chapter demonstrate, effective legal regulation of philanthropy does not end at US borders. American laws regulate international chari-table giving at least as closely as domestic philanthropy. By contrast, the laws gover-ning international philanthropy do not offer nearly as much encouragement for such activity as do their counterpart laws regulating domestic activity. The deductibility rules offer perhaps the starkest illustration of the restrictive shift in applicable laws as philanthropists venture abroad.

---

260   Many other areas of United States law importantly affect international philanthropy but lie beyond the scope of this paper. For example, philanthropic support for foreign charitable organizations may be subject to the Foreign Corrupt Practices Act (15 USC secs. 78dd-1, *et seq.*). *See* Keith M. Korenchuk, et al., *Guarding Against Anti-Corruption Problems in Overseas Philanthropic Activities*, TAXATION OF EXEMPTS, Nov./Dec. 2011, 19, 21 (discussing the potential illegality of charitable gifts made for the purpose of improperly influencing government officials to attract or retain business).

I. The General Disallowance of Individual and Corporate Income Tax Deductions

1. Restrictions on Deductibility for Individuals

As discussed in Chapter Two, Code section 170(c)(2) generally provides for a deduction from taxable income for contributions or gifts to or for the use of charitable organizations. Nevertheless, the deduction is jurisdictionally driven.[261] As part of the conjunctive components of the definition of a charitable organization to which gifts and contributions may be deductible, Code section 170(c)(2)(A) requires such an entity to be *"created or organized in the United States* or in any possession thereof, *or under the law of the United States,* any State, the District of Columbia, or any possession of the United States" (emphases added).

Accordingly, individuals (and corporations) generally may not deduct a gift to or for the use of a charitable organization that was formed neither in the United States nor under United States law. Presumably, a charity could be formed under United States law by United States soldiers stationed in Afghanistan to provide assistance to widows and families of American soldiers killed in combat, and charitable gifts to such an organization would be eligible for deductibility under the latter alternative in Code section 170(c)(2)(A).

Only a few, very limited exceptions exist to this general rule of non-deductibility for charitable gifts to foreign organizations, and they generally may be found in tax treaties negotiated between the United States and foreign governments. Currently, treaties provide for deductibility under United States tax law to organizations formed under the laws of only three foreign countries: Canada, Mexico, and Israel.[262] Each of these treaties contains specific limitations on deductibility, and a full examination of their provisions is beyond the scope of this book. Importantly, however, deductibility under each treaty generally requires (among other things) that the U.S. taxpayer not only make a contribution to an organization that would meet the exemption requirements under United States law, but that the taxpayer also have some source of income

---

261   *See* Victoria B. Bjorklund and Joanna Pressman, "Cross-Border Philanthropy," in Penina Kessler Lieber and Donald R. Levy, eds., *Complete Guide to Nonprofit Organizations* (Civic Research Institute, 2005), at p. 10-10 ("the law allows taxpayers who rely on Section 170 ... to qualify to claim deductions based on the locality in which the charitable organization was organized").

262   *See* Article XXI, Section 5, A Convention Between the United States of America and Canada with Respect to Taxes on Income and on Capital, effective as of January 1, 1985; Article 22, Section 2, The Convention Between the Government of the United States of America and the Government of the United Mexican States for the Avoidance of Double Taxation and the Prevention of Fiscal Evasion with Respect to Taxes on Income, Together with a Related Protocol, effective as of January 1, 1994; and Convention between the Government of the United States of America and the Government of the State of Israel with Respect to Taxes on Income, Protocol 1, Article X, executed on May 30 and June 2, 1980 (all available at http://unclefed.com/ForTaxProfs/Treaties/index.html) (web site last visited on March 3, 2013).

in the foreign country.[263] Aside from these three very limited instances, charitable contributions to organizations formed under the laws of other countries generally are not deductible for individuals under United States income tax law.[264]

This geographic limitation on the deductibility of individual charitable contributions can be traced back to the passage of the Revenue Act of 1938.[265] Legislative history indicates that Congress intended to allow deductions only where private funds would replace obligations that otherwise would have been undertaken by the federal government.[266] The House Ways and Means Committee articulated the following rationale for imposing this domestic restriction on the charitable contribution deduction:

> The exemption from taxation of money or property devoted to charitable and other purposes is based upon the theory that the Government is compensated for the loss of revenue by its *relief from financial burden which would otherwise have to be met by appropriations from public funds, and by the benefits resulting from the promotion of the general welfare. The United States derives no such benefit from gifts to foreign institutions*, and the proposed limitation is consistent with the above theory. If the recipient, however, is a domestic organization the fact that some portion of its funds is used in other countries for charitable and other purposes (such as missionary and educational purposes) will not affect the deductibility of the gift.[267]

The strikingly isolationist tone of this passage underscores that the logic of this domestic limitation on deductions has long since become obsolete in light of the United States' integrated, arguably dominant, role on the world stage, which indeed has undergone several evolutions in the decades since 1938.

Notably, the restriction on the deductibility of gifts to foreign charitable organizations for individual income tax purposes does not translate to the federal laws of estate and gift taxation. Individual charitable gifts to foreign entities made through

---

263   *See* Internal Revenue Service Publication 526, *Charitable Contributions* (2011), at p. 3.
264   Individuals with sufficient financial and administrative capacity could create private foundations with tax-deductible dollars, and those foundations could make grants to foreign charities subject to the expenditure responsibility or equivalency determination rules discussed in detail later in this chapter. Of course, very few individuals have the wherewithal to create and administer private foundations, and such foundations are subject to many other onerous operational restrictions, as discussed in Chapter Two.
265   H.R. 9682, 75th Cong., Pub. L. 75-554 (1938).
266   Bruce R. Hopkins, *The Tax Law of Charitable Giving*, 4th ed. (John Wiley & Sons, 2010), at p. 600.
267   H.R. Rep. No. 1860, 75th Cong., 3d Sess. 19-20 (1938) (emphasis added) (as quoted in Hopkins, *The Tax Law of Charitable Giving, supra* note 266, at pp. 600-01. The final portion of this quoted excerpt highlights a distinction in tax law that persists to this day: the allowance of deductions for charitable gifts to United States "intermediary" organizations that use such gifts partially or wholly outside the United States. Section III of this chapter contains a further discussion of this distinction.

bequests are fully deductible subject to the rules set forth in Code section 2055(a)(2) and the federal regulations promulgated thereunder.[268] Similarly, gifts to foreign charities are fully deductible from amounts subject to the federal gift tax under Code section 2522(a)(2) and the accompanying federal regulations.[269]

2.   Restrictions on Deductibility for Corporations

Corporations engaged in international philanthropy labor under the same general restrictions applicable to their individual counterparts,[270] with one additional limitation. Whereas individuals may deduct charitable gifts to qualified United States organizations that use such gifts to accomplish charitable work outside the United States, corporations may not deduct such gifts unless the donee is a *corporation* formed in the United States or under United States law.[271]

Corporations do have the option of forming private foundations, which are permitted to make grants to foreign charities if they comply with the detailed rules regarding expenditure responsibility or equivalency determinations, which are explained in some detail later in this chapter.[272] Of course, such private foundations (like foundations founded by individuals and families) also are subject to the array of rules discussed in Chapter Two. Accordingly, the private foundation alternative may not be palatable, particularly to a small corporation with a limited philanthropy budget. Multinational corporations also may wish to consider making foreign charitable gifts through their subsidiaries or affiliates located in the countries in question. The deductibility of such gifts would be determinable pursuant to the tax rules of the countries under whose laws the respective subsidiaries or affiliates are formed.[273]

Corporations' ability to deduct charitable gifts to foreign organizations – like that of individuals – is virtually prohibited under rules formulated nearly 75 years ago in an era of United States isolationism. Such rules predate World War II, the advent of the United Nations, the adoption of the Bretton Woods institutions featuring the United States at the formational and operational center, and the rise of longstanding foreign aid programs provided through institutionalized federal agencies such as the United States Agency for International Development.

---

268   *See also* Hopkins, *The Tax Law of Charitable Giving, supra* note 266, at pp. 612-16 for further discussion of international charitable giving by estates.

269   *See also id.* at p. 617.

270   *See* Code section 170(c)(2)(A), which applies the general jurisdictional limitation to both individual and corporate taxpayers.

271   *See* "flush-left" language of Code section 170(c)(2), which provides in part that "[a] contribution or gift by a corporation to a trust, chest, fund, or foundation shall be deductible by reason of this paragraph *only if it is to be used within the United States or any of its possessions* exclusively for [exempt] purposes" (emphasis added).

272   For a helpful overview of the use of company foundations in international grant making, *see generally* Hopkins, *The Tax Law of Charitable Giving, supra* note 266, at pp. 622, *et seq.*

273   *See id.* at p. 620.

As will be discussed at length in Chapter Six, such rules seem archaic in a globa-lized world in which the United States plays leading (even if not always hegemonic) roles in trade, international monetary policy, security, promotion of civil society, and humanitarian relief. Yet private international philanthropy may be facilitated through two other significant (albeit less direct) channels: private foundations and United States public charities that engage in or support foreign charity. These avenues are examined in the following two sections.

II.   International Grants by Private Foundations

1.   Introductory Overview of the Legal Framework

For private foundations seeking to make charitable grants to foreign entities, the two primary considerations under United States law are the minimum annual payout re-quirement[274] and the rules that characterize grants to certain recipients as taxable expenditures unless the foundation exercises expenditure responsibility.[275] In the in-ternational sphere, private foundations must take extra measures if they wish for their grants to constitute "qualifying distributions" under the minimum payout rules and, in all cases, foundations must comply with additional rules to avoid taxable expenditure liability.

To count foreign grants as qualifying distributions, private foundations must follow prescribed guidelines for determining the status of foreign grantees as equi-valents of U.S. public charities.[276] Similarly, for purposes of avoiding liability for taxable expenditure-related excise taxes, foundations making foreign grants must either make the same "equivalency determination" required for purposes of counting such grants as qualifying distributions, or they must exercise expenditure responsibility under Code section 4945(h).[277]

---

274   *See* Code section 4942 and the discussion in section III(4)(b) of Chapter Two.

275   *See* Code section 4945(d)(4) and the discussion in section II(3) of this chapter. Pursuant to Code section 4945(d)(5), taxable expenditures also include grants made for non-charitable purposes. In the absence of a determination that a foreign recipient is the equivalent of an American public charity or the exercise of expenditure responsibility to confirm a charitable use by the grantee, a foreign grant arguably would constitute a taxable expenditure under Code sections 4945(d)(4) *and* (5). *See also* Hopkins, *The Tax Law of Charitable Giving, supra* note 266, at pp. 622-23 (discussing this dual exposure to liability for taxable expenditures).

276   For a helpful overview of the equivalency requirement under Code section 4942, see, e.g., Thomas J. Schenkelberg and Virginia C. Gross, "Private Foundations – Distributions (Section 4942)," 880-2nd Tax Mgmt. (BNA) Estates, Gifts, and Trusts, at A-1 (2004), pp. A-26, *et seq.*

277   *See* Victoria B. Bjorklund and Joanna Pressman, "Cross-Border Philanthropy," in Penina Kessler Lieber and Donald R. Levy, eds., *Complete Guide to Nonprofit Organizations* (Civic Research Institute, 2005), at p. 10-35. Notably, the relationship between the qualifying distribution rules and the taxable expenditure rules is such that a private foundation's foreign grant theoretically could avoid taxable expenditure treatment but still not constitute a qualifying distribution if the foundation does not make an appropriate equivalency determination and also does not require the grantee to maintain the grant proceeds in a segregated fund held for exclusively charitable purposes. *See id.* at p. 10-36 (citing Letter from the IRS to John A. Edie, Esq., Senior Vice President and General Counsel, Council on Foundations,

In light of this general legal framework, a private foundation seeking to make a foreign grant therefore should engage in a two-step inquiry. First, the foundation should determine whether the proposed grantee has obtained an affirmative ruling or determination of public charity classification from the IRS; if so, the grant generally will constitute a qualifying distribution and will not subject the grantor to liability as a taxable expenditure.[278] Very few foreign entities, however, will meet this criterion; one leading commentator suggests that only approximately 500 foreign organizations have even sought such a ruling or determination.[279] Accordingly, in most cases, a private foundation must proceed to the second step: deciding whether to make an equivalency determination or to exercise expenditure responsibility.[280]

2.   Making an Equivalency Determination

Determining that a foreign organization constitutes the equivalent of a United States public charity requires familiarity with a daunting list of statutory and regulatory requirements, as well as time- and labor-intensive inquiries into the proposed grantee's organizational structure and activities. Although by no means easy, the process fortunately has been summarized in a procedure published by the IRS in 1992.

Revenue Procedure ("Rev. Proc.") 92-94, 1992-1 C.B. 507, synthesizes the various provisions of the Internal Revenue Code and federal regulations that apply to the determination of a foreign grantee's public charity classification for purposes of Code sections 4942 and 4945(d)(4). The equivalency determination process in Rev. Proc. 92-94 features two main steps: a "reasonable judgment" of 501(c)(3) equivalency and a "good faith determination" of public charity equivalency.[281] By completing these steps,

---

Apr. 18, 2001).

278   Additionally, a private foundation's grant to a foreign government generally will constitute a qualifying distribution and will avoid taxable expenditure responsibility exposure, so long as the grant is used exclusively for a charitable purpose. Bruce R. Hopkins, *The Tax Law of Charitable Giving*, 4th ed. (John Wiley & Sons, 2010), at p. 626. Verifying a foreign government's exclusively charitable use of grant proceeds, of course, could under some circumstances present unique investigative challenges.

279   *Id.* at p. 627.

280   For a succinct summary of the three scenarios in which a private foundation's foreign grant will constitute a qualifying distribution and will not be treated as a taxable expenditure, *see* Bjorklund and Pressman, "Cross-Border Philanthropy," *supra* note 277, at p. 10-36 (summarizing guidance provided in Letter from the IRS to John A. Edie, Esq., Senior Vice President and General Counsel, Council on Foundations, April 18, 2001).

281   The two steps are identified and discussed at greater length in Michael I. Sanders and Celia Roady, "Private Foundations – Taxable Expenditures (Sec. 4945)," 474 Tax Mgmt. (BNA) Estates, Gifts, and Trusts (2011) at pp. A-59, *et seq.* Importantly, the authors opine that the equivalency determination process arguably may not be available to a private foundation seeking to make a grant to a foreign organization that receives more than 15 percent of its financial support from United States sources (noting that Treas. Reg. sec. 53.4948-1(b) only provides an exemption from the requirement to establish exempt status by filing Form 1023 for foreign organizations that receive at least 85 percent of their support from foreign sources). *Id.* at p. A-61. If these authors are correct, foreign organizations that develop and maintain strong funding relationships with American donors inadvertently could jeopardize their eligibility for funding from private foundations in the United States if they do not affirmatively apply for exemption via Form 1023.

a private foundation may conclude with confidence that its grants to foreign organizations may "be treated as qualifying distributions for purposes of [Code] section 4942 ... rather than as taxable expenditures for purposes of [Code] section 4945."[282]

a.   The "reasonable judgment"

The first requirement outlined in Rev. Proc. 92-94 stems from the rule essentially prohibiting private foundations from making grants for non-charitable purposes. Here, the federal regulations provide that a foreign grantee will be treated as a Code section 501(c)(3) organization, thereby avoiding the additional due diligence required in the regulations to ensure a charitable purpose for the grant, "if in the *reasonable judgment* of a foundation manager of the transferor private foundation the grantee organization is an organization described in section 501(c)(3)."[283] Rev. Proc. 92-94 clarifies that a "reasonable judgment" regarding a foreign grantee's Code section 501(c)(3) equivalency may be based on a qualifying affidavit of the grantee, as described below.[284]

b.   The "good faith determination"

The second requirement of Rev. Proc. 92-94 relates to both the qualifying distribution rule and the general prohibition on private foundation grants to non-public charities (without expenditure responsibility) under the taxable expenditure rules. As to qualifying distributions, the regulations provide that in the absence of a determination or ruling from the IRS, a foreign organization may be treated as a public charity if the grantor foundation "has made a *good faith determination* that the donee organization is an organization described in [Code] section 509(a)(1), (2), or (3)," *i.e.*, that the proposed grantee is a public charity.[285] The regulations further provide that such a "good faith determination" requires an affidavit from the proposed grantee, or an opinion of counsel to either the grantor or the grantee, that the grantee is a public charity.[286]

---

282   Rev. Proc. 92-94, sec. 1.

283   Treas. Reg. sec. 53.4945-6(c)(2)(ii) (emphasis added). For purposes of the rules governing taxable expenditures and qualifying distributions, "foundation managers" include officers, directors, trustees, and others with similar authority and duties, as well as certain employees with authority or responsibility in the area in question, *e.g.*, decisions on grant making. *See* Code sec. 4946(b).

284   Rev. Proc. 92-94, sec. 4.01.

285   Treas. Reg. sec. 53.4942(a)-3(a)(6)(i) (emphasis added).

286   *Id.* On September 24, 2012, the IRS proposed amendments to these regulations that would allow a private foundation to rely on the "good faith determination" not only of its own legal counsel but also of any "qualified tax practitioner," including certain attorneys, certified public accountants, and enrolled agents as described in Treasury Department Circular No. 230. United States Department of the Treasury, Reliance Standards for Making Good Faith Determinations, 77 Fed. Reg. 185 (proposed Sep. 24, 2012) (to be codified at 26 C.F.R. pt. 53). The IRS's explanation of the proposed regulations indicates that this change is designed to "decrease the cost of seeking professional advice regarding [equivalency] determinations, enabling foundations to engage in international philanthropy in a more cost-effective manner [while] encourag[ing] more private foundations to obtain written tax advice, thus promoting the quality of the determinations being made." *Id.* The IRS also suggests in its proposed regulations that it is "considering whether it is appropriate to further amend the current regulations to remove the ability of a private foundation to base a good faith determination on an affidavit of a

Similarly, with respect to the rule under Code section 4945(d)(5) treating grants to non-public charities as taxable expenditures in the absence of expenditure responsibility, the regulations state that a foreign organization lacking an IRS determination or ruling may be treated as a public charity "if the grantor private foundation has made a *good faith determination* that the grantee organization is an organization described in [Code] section 509(a)(1), (2), or (3)."[287] As under the qualifying distribution rules, the taxable expenditure regulations further provide that the "good faith determination" may be based on the proposed grantee's affidavit or an opinion of counsel to the grantor or the grantee.[288]

c.   *Tying it all together: making reasonable judgments and good faith determinations using "currently qualified affidavits"*

Affidavits supporting the "reasonable judgment" and "good faith determination" required by the various regulations discussed above must include the content set forth in section 5 of Rev. Proc. 92-94 and must meet the "currently qualified" guidelines set forth in sections 4.02 through 4.05 of Rev. Proc. 92-94.[289] For grantee-prepared affidavits, a "principal officer" of the grantee – such as the chairman of the board, chief executive officer, or executive director – must execute the affidavit.[290] Importantly, the affidavit must be written in English, and supporting documentation written in other languages must be translated into English[291] – a potentially burdensome requirement for foreign grantees lacking personnel with English language skills or translation resources.

As to content requirements, the grantee's attesting officer must address several general areas of information. These content areas include an identification of the officer's title; the year of the grantee's organization and an identification of the charitable or other exempt purposes for which it is exclusively operated; a description of the grantee's past, current, and future activities; the attachment of the grantee's "charter" (*e.g.*, articles of incorporation), bylaws, and other governance documents; a prescribed statement to the effect that the laws governing the grantee do not permit private inurement of its income or assets, more than an insubstantial amount of lobby-

---

foreign grantee, which may be a less reliable basis for making a good faith determination than advice from a qualified tax practitioner." *Id.* The IRS established December 24, 2012, as the deadline for submitting comments and requests for hearing on the proposed regulations. *Id.* As of February 26, 2013, no further update on these proposed regulations was available.

287   Treas. Reg. sec. 53.4945-5(a)(5) (emphasis added).

288   *Id.* The proposed regulations on qualifying distributions that were issued by the IRS on September 24, 2012, also would amend this regulatory provision by allowing good faith determinations to be based on opinions of "qualified tax practitioner[s]." United States Department of the Treasury, Reliance Standards for Making Good Faith Determinations, 77 Fed. Reg. 185 (proposed Sep. 24, 2012) (to be codified at 26 C.F.R. pt. 53).

289   See Rev. Proc. 92-94, secs. 5.01 and 4.01, respectively.

290   Rev. Proc. 92-94, sec. 5.01.

291   *Id.*

ing, more than an insubstantial amount of non-charitable activities, or any political campaign activity (all parallel to the restrictions in Code section 501(c)(3)); verification that no shareholders or members hold proprietary (pecuniary) interests in the grantee; assurance that upon dissolution, the grantee's assets will be distributed for permissible charitable or other exempt purposes (including the attachment of the controlling provision in the grantee's governance documents or a copy of an applicable statute requiring such distribution upon dissolution); identification of any organizations that control the grantee or in connection with which the grantee is operated; and, where appropriate, a financial schedule containing information designed to demonstrate that the grantee can satisfy one of the public support tests set forth in Code section 509(a)(1) and (2).[292]

To be "currently qualified," the preceding facts either must be accurate as of the grantee's most recently completed taxable year or updated to reflect current information.[293] Updates may be provided either with an attested financial statement, where applicable (e.g., four prior years of public support information for a grantee whose public charity equivalency depends on establishing sufficiently broad public support), or with an attested statement confirming that the pertinent facts have not changed (where the grantee's public charity equivalency depends on non-financial factors such as operation of a school or a church).[294]

By obtaining a currently qualified affidavit that meets each of the foregoing requirements for content and contemporaneousness, a private foundation will be able to treat a grant to a foreign organization as a qualifying distribution, thereby counting toward the foundation's annual minimum payout requirement under Code section 4942, and will be assured that the grant is not a taxable expenditure under Code section 4945(d)(4), thereby obviating any need to exercise expenditure responsibility under Code section 4945(h). The equivalency determination procedure in Rev. Proc. 92-94 therefore constitutes a useful tool for private foundations regularly engaged in foreign grant making. Moreover, as discussed in Chapter Six, the equivalency determination could be put to greater use for private foundations by combining current capabilities in communications technology with a slightly more permissive legal regime, and such improvements also could be adapted – with appropriate revisions to current deductibility restrictions – to encourage greater and more effective involvement in international philanthropy by individuals and corporations.

---

[292]   See id., sec. 5.04(1)-(11). Additional requirements apply to grantees that claim classification as a school or an operating foundation. See id., secs. 5.03 and 5.04(12) and (13).

[293]   Id., sec. 4.03.

[294]   Id., secs. 4.04 and 4.05.

3.   The Role of Expenditure Responsibility

Private foundations may avoid taxable expenditure treatment under Code section 4945(d)(4) for grants to foreign organizations even if they opt not to undertake an equivalency determination as described in Rev. Proc. 92-94. An alternative approach proceeds from the assumption that the foreign organization is not a public charity, and it involves following the expenditure responsibility procedures required by Code section 4945(d)(4)(B) for grants to non-public charities.[295]

The expenditure responsibility rules are designed to provide greater assurance that a grant to a non-charity will be used for the charitable purposes intended by a private foundation grantor. Nevertheless, the rules expressly state that a private foundation is not an "insurer" of a grantee's charitable activity; rather, a foundation must only "[exert] all reasonable efforts and [establish] adequate procedures" in that regard.[296]

A foundation's "efforts and ... procedures" must be designed to accomplish three objectives: seeing that its grant is used solely for its intended charitable purposes; obtaining sufficient reports from the grantee regarding its expenditure of the grant; and making sufficient reports to the IRS regarding the grantee's expenditures.[297] These objectives, in turn, will be satisfied if the foundation completes four discrete tasks: conducting a pre-grant inquiry into the proposed grantee's history, management, activities, and practices;[298] executing a grant agreement that contains terms and conditions required by the regulations;[299] obtaining annual written reports from the grantee regarding its use of the grant proceeds, compliance with the terms of the grant agreement, and progress toward accomplishing the charitable purposes of the

---

295   See Victoria B. Bjorklund and Joanna Pressman, "Cross-Border Philanthropy," in Penina Kessler Lieber and Donald R. Levy, eds., *Complete Guide to Nonprofit Organizations* (Civic Research Institute, 2005), p. 10-35 (a private foundation may "bypass the good-faith equivalency determination procedure and, instead, treat the grantee as a non-charity from the outset and turn directly to expenditure responsibility"). As noted earlier, expenditure responsibility only solves the taxable expenditure dilemma; it does not necessarily ensure that a grant will constitute a qualifying distribution under Code section 4942. *See supra* note 277.

296   Treas. Reg. sec. 53.4945-5(b)(1), promulgated pursuant to Code sec. 4945(h).

297   *See* Code sec. 4945(h)(1)-(3).

298   *See* Treas. Reg. sec. 53.4945-5(b)(2).

299   *See* Treas. Reg. sec. 53.4945-5(b)(3)(i)-(iv) (requiring the grantee to repay proceeds not used for the charitable purposes specified in the grant agreement, submit annual reports on grant expenditures, maintain financial records related to the grant and make such records available to the foundation, and refrain from using the grant proceeds for lobbying, political campaigning, redistributions for certain travel or study purposes or to non-public charities, or any non-charitable purpose).

grant;[300] and reporting certain grant-related information to the IRS on the foundation's annual return (Form 990-PF).[301]

The expenditure responsibility rules are extensive, and the regulations offer far more special rules and exceptions that need not be discussed herein. In light of the time and resources required to satisfy the rules, many private foundations categorically refuse to make grants to non-public charities, particularly in the domestic context. Internationally, however, the expenditure responsibility framework may offer a useful alternative to private foundations, particularly those that are strongly committed to supporting certain charitable, educational, or religious programs overseas even if such programs are not carried out by public charities.

As is the case with equivalency determinations, the expenditure responsibility rules impose significant recordkeeping and reporting burdens on foreign grantees. Before making foreign grants, therefore, private foundations would be well advised to consider the extent of such burdens and the grantee's access to (and, in some cases, ability to pay for) compliance-related resources to the grantee, including individuals with bookkeeping, technical writing, and/or translation skills. Private foundations also could help foreign grantees meet these special challenges by obtaining information on local resources in the grantees' respective localities, connecting grantees to such resources, and perhaps even adding technical support components to overall grant amounts in order to promote compliance efforts by grantees (which, in turn, promote foundations' interests in satisfying expenditure responsibility and/or equivalency determination requirements).

4.   Other Contemporary Legal Factors Affecting International Grant Making by Private Foundations

As if the intricate applicability rules and substantive requirements associated with equivalency determinations and expenditure responsibility were not complicated enough, private foundations seeking to engage in foreign grant making also must stay abreast of other legal developments uniquely affecting cross-border philanthropic activity. Two of the most significant current developments in this regard involve (a) the constantly evolving restrictions and guidelines related to international terrorism and illicit activities and (b) the recently proposed regulations that would clarify the permis-

---

300   *See* Treas. Reg. sec. 53.4945-5(c)(1).

301   *See* Treas. Reg. sec. 53.4945-5(d)(1). Each such report on Form 990-PF must include the grantee's name and address, the date on which the grant was made, the amount of the grant, the amounts expended to date by the grantee, a description of any known diversions of proceeds by the grantee away from the charitable purposes of the grant, the date(s) on which the grantee provided its required annual report(s), and any results of annual report verification efforts undertaken by the foundation. *See* Treas. Reg. sec. 53.4945-5(d)(2)(i)-(vii).

sibility of certain international "program-related investments" by private foundations.[302]

a.   *The problems of terrorism and illicit activities in international philanthropy*

The terrorist attacks of September 11, 2001, resulted in countless reformulations of
American foreign security policy, embodied in new statutes, regulations, executive
orders, and administrative agency guidelines at the federal and state levels, and even
the creation of wholly new agencies such as the United States Department of Home-
land Security. Philanthropy – particularly in the international context – also witnessed
the development of new and increased compliance rules designed to ensure that
Americans' tax-deductible charitable contributions are not used to finance terrorist
activities against the American people. As a primary source of American philanthropy
abroad, private foundations must pay particular attention to developments on this
front.

    Pursuant to Executive Order 13224 (Sep. 23, 2001), signed less than two weeks
after the 9/11 attacks, charitable contributions are among the types of transactions
prohibited between United States citizens and any individual or entity (including a
government) identified in one of several lists or associated with a listed person.[303] Such
lists of "specially designated nationals" are maintained by the Department of
Treasury's Office of Foreign Assets Control ("OFAC") and are available online.[304] Private
foundations engaged in international grant making should become familiar with the
OFAC lists and consult the most recent versions of the lists before agreeing to make
grants to foreign organizations (or, indeed, to domestic organizations engaged in
foreign activities or even certain domestic activities that reasonably could raise security concerns; in short, to virtually any proposed grantee).

    In addition to the OFAC lists of specially designated nationals, private foun-
dations making foreign grants also should familiarize themselves with the Department
of the Treasury's Anti-Terrorist Financing Guidelines. These guidelines are voluntary,
rather than mandatory, but they reflect updated best practices for foundations seeking
to guard against the inadvertent financing of terrorism and to investigate the accountability and transparency of proposed grantees in the areas of governance and

---

302   An additional challenge for private foundations, which is not discussed in this book, centers on the
        extent to which foundations must withhold and remit United States federal income taxes from
        payments of grants to foreign individuals or entities where such grants support activities conducted
        in the United States. *See* Treas. Reg. secs. 1.1441-1 through 1.1441-9.

303   *See* Janne G. Gallagher, "Grantmaking in an Age of Terrorism: Some Thoughts about Compliance Stra-
        tegies," 70 International Dateline (Council on Foundations, 2004) (available at http://www.cof.org/tem-
        plates/content.cfm?itemnumber=12696&navItemNumber=15633), at text accompanying n.7.

304   *See* United States Department of the Treasury, Office of Foreign Assets Control, Specially Designated
        Nationals List, http://www.treasury.gov/resource-center/sanctions/SDN-List/Pages/default.aspx (web
        site last visited on March 3, 2013).

finance.[305] OFAC also provides a helpful "Risk Matrix for the Charitable Sector" designed to assist charities engaged in foreign activity (and those who support them) in avoiding risks related to international terrorism and other illegal activities such as narcotics trafficking.[306] Private foundations engaged in international grant making should consult these resources regularly to minimize the risk of their involvement with terrorist or other illegal activities abroad.

b.   *International program-related investments for private foundations*

The seemingly omnipresent threats associated with terrorism and illicit activities represent an unfortunate fact of life for any actor engaged in the international sphere. Happily, another significant contemporary development addresses the more positive subject of creative investments by private foundations in aspects of international development. This topic initially requires a basic familiarity with the program-related investment rules applicable to private foundations.

Program-related investments ("PRIs") are defined in the jeopardy investment rules under Code section 4944[307] with two significant requirements: the primary purpose of the investment must be the accomplishment of one or more charitable, educational, or other exempt purposes; and no significant purpose of the investment may be the production of income or the appreciation of property.[308] If an investment meets these two criteria, it will not be deemed a jeopardy investment that would subject the foundation to excise tax liability.[309] Other favorable treatment is accorded to PRIs under the private foundation rules. PRIs generally constitute qualifying distributions toward a private foundation's minimum payout requirement,[310] and they may be excluded from a private foundation's assets when calculating its minimum payout requirement.[311] Moreover, PRIs generally will not constitute taxable expenditures if the private foundation exercises any required expenditure responsibility.[312] These advantages make PRIs a very attractive complement to traditional grants, particularly for private foundations that wish to effect change in the areas of international development.

---

305   *See generally* United States Department of the Treasury, Anti-Terrorist Financing Guidelines: Voluntary Best Practices for U.S.-Based Charities (available online at http://www.treasury.gov/resource-center/terrorist-illicit-finance/Pages/protecting-charities-intro.aspx) (web site last visited on March 3, 2013).

306   *See generally* United States Department of the Treasury, Risk Matrix for the Charitable Sector (available online at http://www.treasury.gov/resource-center/terrorist-illicit-finance/Pages/protecting-index.aspx) (last visited on March 3, 2013).

307   *See also* the discussion of jeopardy investments in section III(4)(f) of Chapter Two.

308   *See* Code sec. 4944(c).

309   *Id.*

310   *See* Treas. Reg. sec. 53.4942(a)-3(a)(2)(i).

311   *See* Treas. Reg. sec. 53.4942(a)-2(c)(3)(ii)(*d*).

312   *See* Treas. Reg. secs. 53.4945-5(b)(4) and 53.4945-6(c)(1)(i).

In April 2012, the Department of Treasury issued proposed regulations that, if ultimately adopted, would clarify that several areas of international activity constitute PRIs and thus generally would qualify for the favorable treatment described above in connection with the rules governing required minimum payouts, jeopardy investments, and taxable expenditures.[313] Technically, the proposed regulations only address whether investments constitute jeopardy investments under Code section 4944, but they note that the PRI illustrated in one example involving a loan guarantee and reimbursement arrangement would not constitute a qualifying distribution under Code section 4942.[314] Accordingly, if the proposed regulations are adopted in their current form, private foundations should carefully analyze the treatment of PRIs covered by the new examples as qualifying distributions, and such analysis should reflect a consideration of the factors discussed in the individual examples. Nevertheless, the proposed regulations have generated excitement among those who seek a more entrepreneurial role for philanthropy.[315]

The proposed regulations would add nine examples of PRIs to the ten currently listed in the federal regulations.[316] Several of the examples contemplate investments (including, in some cases, below-market loans) in enterprises engaged in endeavors affecting developing countries, including the development of drugs to prevent diseases prevalent in such countries; the collection and delivery to recycling centers of solid waste generated in remote locations; the starting of small businesses in areas recently impacted by natural disasters; and the financing of purchasing programs with indigent coffee farmers that promote improved management of water, cultivation of crops, and pest management practices.[317] At least one professional advisor has opined that the regulations could, for example, clarify the permissibility of a "long shot equity investment in an orphan drug research company" even where long-term financial returns are possible.[318]

---

313   United States Department of the Treasury, Examples of Program-Related Investments, 77 Fed. Reg. 23429 (proposed Apr. 19, 2012) (to be codified at 26 C.F.R. pt. 53). The proposed regulations called for the submission of comments and public hearing requests by July 18, 2012. As of February 26, 2013, no further update on the proposed regulations was available.

314   *Id.*

315   *See, e.g.,* Robert C. Pozen, *Why Not Venture-Capital Philanthropy?,* WALL STREET JOURNAL (June 3, 2012) (available online at http://online.wsj.com/article/SB10001424052702304840904577422430641379116.html).

316   The existing examples appear in Treas. Reg. sec. 53.4944-3(b).

317   *See* 77 Fed. Reg. 23429, Examples 11-12 and 15-16.

318   Diane Freda, *Program-Related Investments Guidance Clears Up International, Other PRI Issues,* BLOOMBERG BNA DAILY TAX REPORT, May 1, 2012 (quoting attorney Ofer Lion). Mr. Lion appeared to be referring to the drug development scenario in Example 11 while noting the IRS's reference to Example 12 in the "Explanation of Provisions" section of the proposed regulations, which describes the high risks but potentially high yields associated with the recycling program investment contemplated therein. *See also IRS Rules Would Allow Private Foundations to Make Range of Charitable Investments,* BLOOMBERG BNA DAILY TAX REPORT, Apr. 19, 2012 (citing preamble's reference to "[o]ne example illustrat[ing] that the existence of a high potential rate of return on an investment does not, by itself, prevent the investment from qualifying as a PRI").

The proposed regulations do not constitute new policy; rather, they reflect clarifications of existing rules regarding the treatment of PRIs.[319] If finalized, the regulations would offer certainty to private foundations seeking to engage in certain international investment activities without incurring the time and expense associated with obtaining a private letter ruling or a formal legal opinion.[320] For private foundations seeking more innovative means to stimulate international economic development as a charitable activity, the proposed regulations offer an encouraging development.

III.   Charitable Gifts to United States Charities for Foreign Use

Thus far in Chapter Three, I have focused on two avenues for international philanthropy by American citizens, as well as the laws that affect those modes of giving. The first approach, direct giving by individuals and corporations, is significantly hampered by the absence of deductibility for such gifts under federal income tax rules. The second, private foundation grant making, is accompanied by a well-developed (and still developing) body of law that facilitates and carefully prescribes international charitable giving with tax-favored dollars, i.e., funds with which tax-deductible contributions previously were made to foundations – although, as noted earlier, private foundations may be beyond the practical reach of most Americans.

The third and final[321] main mode for international giving encompasses contributions to United States public charities that use such gifts to engage in or support charitable activities abroad. Public charities are not precluded from engaging in international activity, and unlike private foundations, their grant making is not subject to the restrictions associated with the qualifying distribution and taxable expenditure rules. With this relatively wide latitude, accompanied by the advantageous deducti-

---

319   A Treasury Department attorney has noted that while the existing regulations did not prohibit foreign PRIs, all of the existing examples featured domestic scenarios. Diane Freda, *Program-Related Investment Guidance Adds More Current Examples for Exempts*, BLOOMBERG BNA DAILY TAX REPORT, Apr. 20, 2012 (quoting Ruth Madrigal, Treasury Department attorney advisor).

320   *See* Suzanne Perry, *White House Seeks to Spur Innovative Spending by Foundations*, THE CHRONICLE OF PHILANTHROPY/TAX WATCH (May 10, 2012), http://philanthropy.com/article/White-House-Seeks-to-Spur/131840/.

321   Other methods used less frequently in the international context, the discussion of which lies beyond the scope of this book, include the use of donor-advised funds embedded within public charities (*see* discussion in section III(3)(c) in Chapter Two) and "offshore" charitable organizations subject to the laws of foreign countries. In the latter alternative, deductions under U.S. tax law would not be available to the donor. *See* Victoria B. Bjorklund and Joanna Pressman, "Cross-Border Philanthropy," in Penina Kessler Lieber and Donald R. Levy, eds., *Complete Guide to Nonprofit Organizations* (Civic Research Institute, 2005), at p. 10-44. Nina Crimm also observes that individual and corporate gifts to a so-called "bi-national" organization, created under the laws of more than one country, would not be deductible because such an organization would not be created "exclusively" under the laws of the United States pursuant to Code section 170(c)(2)(A). Nina J. Crimm, *Through a Post-September 11 Looking Glass: Assessing the Roles of Federal Tax Laws and Tax Policies Applicable to Global Philanthropy by Private Foundations and Their Donors*, 23 VA. TAX REV. 1, 113 (2003) (citing Rev. Rul. 76-195, 1976-1 C.B. 61).

bility rules discussed in Chapter Two, public charities[322] represent the most attractive current option for individuals and corporations desiring to engage in cross-border philanthropy.

The role of American public charities in receiving charitable gifts domestically and utilizing such gifts internationally has been described as that of an "intermediary."[323] Nevertheless, this intermediary role features one very significant limitation, which relates to the deductibility rules for individuals and corporations under Code section 170. For a gift to the public charity to be deductible, the public charity must be able to exercise control over the gift. Consequently, if a donor requires the public charity to redistribute a gift to a foreign organization or otherwise spend the proceeds of the gift on behalf of a foreign organization, then the original gift will be deemed to have been made for the benefit of a foreign organization and therefore will not be eligible for deduction by reason of the geographic limitation. The IRS expressed this view nearly fifty years ago in an oft-quoted ruling:

> [T]he requirements of section 170(c)(2)(A) of the Code would be nullified if contributions inevitably committed to go to a foreign organization were held to be deductible solely because, in the course of transmittal to the foreign organization, they came to rest momentarily in a qualifying domestic organization. In such cases the domestic organization is only nominally the donee; the real donee is the ultimate foreign recipient.[324]

In the same 1963 ruling, the IRS reviewed five hypothetical scenarios involving distributions from initial domestic recipients to subsequent international recipients. Three of those scenarios reflected structures or schemes in which the domestic charity was a mere conduit, lacking sufficient discretion as to the use of gifts received and retransmitted to foreign recipients, thereby resulting in the disallowance of deductions for donors to the domestic charity.[325] The IRS offered a colorful rationale for the disallowance of deductions in such instances, explaining that "[a] given result at the end of a straight path is not made a different result because reached by following a devious path."[326]

In coordinating solicitations for gifts to support international programs, a public charity therefore must take care not to plot a "devious path" by allowing donors to designate ultimate foreign recipients. Instead, the public charity must retain control over the use of such gifts. The control requirement ensures that a donor is actually

---

322   It bears emphasis that churches, a major source of international giving and charitable programming, constitute public charities under Code section 170(b)(1)(A)(i).

323   *See, e.g.*, Charles R. Ostertag, *We're Starting to Share Well with Others: Cross-Border Giving Lessons from the Court of Justice of the European Union*, 20 TUL. J. INT'L & COMP. L. 255, 272 (2011).

324   Rev. Rul. 63-252, 1963-2 C.B. 101.

325   *Id.* (examples (1), (2), and (3)).

326   *Id.* (quoting *Minnesota Tea Co. v. Helvering*, 302 U.S. 609, 613 (1938)).

supporting an organization established in the United States or under United States law rather than a foreign recipient to which charitable contributions would be non-deductible pursuant to Code section 170(c)(2)(A).[327]

The most commonly utilized method for ensuring a public charity's retention of requisite control is the so-called "American Friends of" organization. In light of the control requirement inherent in the geographic limitation of Code section 170(c)(2)(A), philanthropists and their professional advisors have developed this international solicitation and giving method, which reflects the contours of one of the two per-missible scenarios articulated by the IRS in Rev. Rul. 63-252.[328]

The "American Friends of" organizational model typically is patterned after the IRS's 1966 amplification of its 1963 ruling, which appears in Rev. Rul. 66-79.[329] There, the IRS ruled that where a domestic charity, on its own initiative, reviews and approves proposed grants for specific charitable projects to be undertaken by foreign organi-zations, and where the charity subsequently solicits contributions to support such projects, such contributions will be eligible for deductibility by the donors – so long as the domestic charity retains the right to change course, withdraw its support for the foreign program(s), and use the solicited contributions for other permissible pur-poses.[330]

The IRS has reiterated its approval of similar programs in subsequent rulings. In 1975, the IRS granted a favorable ruling with general precedential value to a domestic charity engaged in plant and wildlife preservation projects in a foreign country. The charity used both its own staff and foreign contractors to manage its projects abroad and made grants to foreign organizations only where, *inter alia*, the domestic charity itself "maintains control and responsibility over the use of any funds granted ... by first making a field investigation of the purposes to which the funds will be put." Under

---

327   The distinctions between United States and foreign charities are not always intuitively apparent. *See, e.g.*, Bruce R. Hopkins, *The Tax Law of Charitable Giving*, 4th ed. (John Wiley & Sons, 2010), at pp. 601-02, discussing *Welti v. Commissioner*, 1 T.C. 905 (1943), in which the Tax Court held that gifts to a church in Switzerland were not deductible under United States law where the Swiss church was affiliated with but not controlled by an American "mother" church, and contrasting *Welti* with the Tax Court's decision in *Bilingual Montessori School of Paris, Inc. v. Commissioner*, 75 T.C. 480 (1980), in which gifts to a Delaware corporation formed by the operators of a French school were held deductible under United States law because the Delaware corporation itself used the funds raised to operate the French school, rather than distributing such funds to a separate foreign operator.

328   Rev. Rul. 63-252 (examples (4) and (5)). The "American Friends of" approaches are summarized well in Bjorklund and Pressman, "Cross-Border Philanthropy," *supra* note 321, at pp. 10-14 through 10-17.

329   1966-1 C.B. 48.

330   *Id.* (the domestic charity may not "accept contributions so earmarked that they must in any event go to the foreign organization ... The test in each case is whether the [domestic] organization has full control of the donated funds, and discretion as to their use").

these facts, the IRS ruled that non-earmarked contributions to the domestic public charity would be deductible under Code section 170.[331]

The key element of any "American Friends of" organization is the retention of discretion by the domestic charity as to its ultimate use of contributions received from American donors. This retained control element ensures that the domestic charity avoids serving as a mere conduit for the deduction of otherwise non-deductible contributions "earmarked" for the benefit of foreign recipients.[332]

Notably, in the 1966 ruling that established the template for "American Friends of" organizations, the governing board of the domestic charity would review and approve particular project requests, after which the charity would conduct fundraising campaigns to support the selected projects. The governing board would retain authority to redirect any funds raised for other projects or purposes.[333] This formula offers different sequential options for a domestic charity interested in facilitating foreign grants. First, the domestic charity could solicit and consider project "wish lists" identified in advance by foreign charities. Alternatively, donors to the domestic charity could initiate suggestions for projects and pledge funds for such projects, contingent upon the domestic charity's approval of those projects.[334]

IV.   Concluding Thoughts on United States Laws Affecting International Philanthropy

International philanthropy by Americans features several channels of giving by individuals and organizations. Individuals and corporations do sometimes give directly to foreign charities, but they do so without the incentive of income tax deductions associated with their gifts. Private foundations also make grants directly to foreign charities, but such grants may be undertaken only in conjunction with the fulfillment of complex due diligence procedures designed to verify a grantee's organizational eligibility and the charitable nature of the activities it will undertake with the funds granted. And finally, individuals and corporations (as well as private foundations) make contributions to United States charities that use such gifts to support or conduct charitable endeavors abroad – but in such instances, the deductibility of individual and corporate contributions to the domestic charity is contingent on the domestic

---

331   Rev. Rul. 76-65, 1975-1 C.B. 79 (citing Rev. Ruls. 63-252 and 66-79). For an example of an IRS analysis applying the same rules but reaching a negative conclusion, *see* General Counsel Memorandum 37444 (March 7, 1978) (deductions for contributions to a domestic public charity not permitted where "it appears that [the domestic charity] is intending to remit the monies to [a foreign grantee] before even considering possible projects and then discussing with [such grantee] the possible uses").

332   The domestic charity may, for example, allow donors to request (but not dictate) that gift be used for a particular recipient or program. Victoria B. Bjorklund and Joanna Pressman, "Cross-Border Philanthropy," in Penina Kessler Lieber and Donald R. Levy, eds., *Complete Guide to Nonprofit Organizations* (Civic Research Institute, 2005), at p. 10-23.

333   Rev. Rul. 66-79, 1966-1 C.B. 48.

334   Bjorklund and Pressman, "Cross-Border Philanthropy," *supra* note 332, at pp. 10-23 through 10-24.

charity's retention of discretion and control regarding the use of the contribution, whether coincidentally for the purpose favored by the donor or for any other domestic or international objective.

In the international context, the robust requirements and restrictions associated with deductibility for individual and corporate contributions, along with requirements governing the permissibility of private foundation grants, ably illustrate the maturity of the United States' legal framework in ensuring that assets receiving favorable tax treatment are indeed used for purposes consistent with the rationale underlying those tax advantages. In this sense, United States laws are well designed and developed to fulfill a regulatory function: they place limits on the uses of tax-deductible dollars in the international context and prevent the use of such funds for any purpose other than those that advance the purposes of American charitable organizations.

On the other hand, while the laws of the United States provide effective restrictions and boundaries to ensure the integrity of international giving, those restrictions and boundaries – both as to deductibility and with respect to private foundation grant making – are not balanced by provisions that adequately encourage Americans to engage in the support of charitable efforts undertaken by *foreign* organizations around the globe. In short, United States laws governing international philanthropy weigh heavily in favor of regulation over encouragement. Moreover, to the extent that United States laws encourage any charitable giving with international effects, they undergird the pursuit of American interests, including the charitable purposes of domestic charities and domestic private foundations; foreign nationals' charitable purposes are promoted only incidentally as a means of furthering Americans' charitable ideals.

It is time for this state of affairs to change. United States citizens live in a globalized world in which the interests of individuals and organizations around the world inherently affect their own. Although American engagement and leadership reflected a core feature of global affairs throughout the latter half of the twentieth century, the rise of emerging world leaders such as China, India, and Brazil – combined with the latent power of Russia and the combined size of the European Union – means that in the twenty-first century the United States no longer occupies unquestioned supremacy in political, economic, or social terms.

Furthermore, largely in light of the markedly more assertive nature of American military engagement during the early years of the current century, the benevolence of American involvement in international affairs is no longer presumed in other quarters, particularly across the Middle East and throughout the Arab world. Even in international development, where the United States traditionally operated as the dominant provider of support for infrastructural projects, educational improvements, and the promotion of civil society, China has aggressively stepped up its efforts to improve conditions in sub-Saharan Africa, Latin America, and other regions where its commercial interests are affected – and such efforts are predictably subject to critiques questioning the extent of China's altruism in this regard.[335]

By encouraging more – and more effective – international philanthropic engagement on the part of American citizens, United States tax law could catch up to the reality of an interconnected world, and it could promote national interests abroad by offering modes of engagement that further different (but often complementary) objectives than those pursued through military actions designed to defend real or perceived security interests or trade and monetary policy designed to protect domestic commercial concerns. And just as importantly, a more permissive legal framework could stimulate Americans to place more of their material resources at the disposal of individuals and organizations around the world to further worthy causes such as education, environmental sustainability, civil society programs, relief from systemic poverty, food insecurity, disease eradication, reconciliation across ethnic and religious groups, and many more.

To be sure, legal structures cannot by themselves change human behavior or transform societies, but they can encourage and promote behaviors that societies view as desirable or useful. The remainder of this book, therefore, sets forth an argument in favor of modest changes in United States tax law that could encourage Americans to increase their level of engagement in international philanthropy and to do so in ways that more directly support the charitable interests of foreign nationals.[336] This exploration will commence in Chapter Four with a brief discussion of the foundational non-legal policy issues that affect philanthropic giving positively and negatively, both domestically and internationally. Transitioning to an exclusively international context in Chapter Five, I identify and discuss arguments supporting philanthropic engagement by Americans that reflects a greater degree of direct support for the charitable efforts of foreign nationals. Finally, in Chapter Six I recommend several modest changes to the United States' legal framework, the current state of which was summarized in Chapters Two and Three. Those recommended changes in the law, in turn, could be designed to address the policy factors and achieve the policy goals outlined in Chapters Four and Five, respectively.

---

335   See. e.g., Howard W. French, The Next Empire, THE ATLANTIC (May 2010), available online at http://www.theatlantic.com/magazine/archive/2010/05/the-next-empire/308018/ (analyzing whether China's development work in Africa reflects primarily "transformation" or "exploitation" objectives).

336   As noted earlier, the term "charitable" as used herein often encompasses educational, religious, scientific, literary, and other related purposes as contemplated in Code sections 170(c)(2)(B) and 501(c)(3).

Chapter Four:

General Policy Matters Affecting Domestic and International Philanthropy

Although the laws of the United States exert significant impact on philanthropy, those laws are written, enforced, observed, and sometimes disregarded in the context of countless policy factors that affect, and to some extent, circumscribe philanthropic activity. While it would be impossible to enumerate an exhaustive list of such factors, this section illustrates a few of the most significant non-legal issues that shape our public discussion of philanthropy and ultimately influence the content of laws that govern charitable giving. These issues are examined first as they affect philanthropy generally, *i.e.*, whether domestically or internationally, and then specifically as they impact international giving.

I.   General Policy Issues Affecting Philanthropy

1.   Personal Motivations for Charitable Giving

It is tempting to speak of philanthropy in an exclusively collective or societal sense, *e.g.*, "American philanthropy" or "private foundation grant making." At the core of every discussion of charitable giving, however – even in an examination of an organization's gift or grant – stands an individual (perhaps in collaboration with one or more others, *e.g.*, in a corporate context) who made a decision to give. In seeking to encourage more and better philanthropy, whether domestically or internationally, it is therefore useful first to discern donors' motives for supporting charitable efforts.

At face value, charitable donors must be motivated at least in part by some desire to better their communities, nations, and world, for in giving they have eschewed other uses of their resources, including investment or consumption, that could more directly and exclusively benefit themselves. Nevertheless, charitable impulses need not always reflect unalloyed altruism. Indeed, social scientist Robert Bellah has noted that for citizens highly engaged in community activism (whether or not in charitable activities), "getting involved" demonstrates not just a "genuine concern for one's local community" but also "the protection of one's interests."[337] School board involvement and participation in homeowners' associations offer but two of the numerous examples of such mixed-motive activism.

Protection of one's own interests animates charitable giving as well as the active engagement analyzed by Bellah. In his seminal study on American society and politics, Alexis de Tocqueville observed that Americans unabashedly acknowledge the

---

337   Robert N. Bellah, et al., *Habits of the Heart: Individualism and Commitment in American Life* (Harper & Row, 1985), at p. 191.

practical necessity of sacrificial private virtue on behalf their fellow citizens.[338] De Tocqueville himself predicted, arguably with prescience, that in increasingly egalitarian societies, all private actions would be motivated principally by such enlightened self-interest.[339] Tax deductions in connection with charitable gifts, of course, represent one type of material self-interest, and studies indicate that tax advantages may partly motivate charitable giving, at least among relatively wealthier donors.[340]

Economist Kenneth Boulding described a "grants economy" and a spectrum of grants reflecting motives from outright gifts on one end to "tribute" on the other.[341] While Boulding posited that taxation represents "coerced grants," others see taxes reflecting a fee-for-service exchange between private citizens and government.[342] Grants, i.e., private philanthropic giving, can be construed in similar fashion. Even if one agrees with Robert Reich that philanthropy constitutes a form of consumption,[343] such consumption would seem to manifest something other (or at least more) than a purely selfish desire for personal material betterment.

In economic terms, philanthropy at the very least comprises a relatively inefficient means of achieving personal protection or advancement, and it creates positive externalities. In a more affirmative sense, however, it can be – and has been – argued that philanthropy expresses the donor's "sense of community with others."[344] This community, or identification, between giver and recipient represents precisely the

---

338 Alexis de Tocqueville, *Democracy in America* (Penguin Books translation, 2003), at 610 ("American moralists ... do not ... deny that every man can pursue his own self-interest but they turn themselves inside out to prove that it is in each man's interest to be virtuous"). *See also* Jeffrey D. Sachs, *The Price of Civilization: Reawakening American Virtue and Prosperity* (Random House, 2011), at p. 168 (citing psychologist Daniel Gilbert for the proposition that more happiness may be derived from income by using it "to help others instead of ourselves, because as hypersocial animals, 'almost anything we do to improve our connections with others tends to improve our happiness as well'," quoting Elizabeth Dunn, et al., *If Money Doesn't Make You Happy Then You Probably Aren't Spending It Right*, JOURNAL OF CONSUMER PSYCHOLOGY 21, no. 2, at p. 123).

339 De Tocqueville, *supra* note 338, at 612-13.

340 *See* Center on Philanthropy at Indiana University, *The 2010 Study of High Net Worth Philanthropy* (2010), available at http://www.philanthropy.iupui.edu/research-by-category/the-2010-study-of-high-net-worth-philanthropy, at p. 47 (reporting responses of survey participants generally indicating that their philanthropic giving would decrease in the absence of tax deductibility in connection with such giving).

341 Steven D. Ealy, Research Note, *Taxation as a One-Way Transfer? A Note on a Conceptual Confusion in Kenneth Boulding*, 4 CONVERSATIONS ON PHILANTHROPY 47, 48 (Donors Trust, 2007) (quoting Kenneth Boulding, *The Economy of Love and Fear: A Preface to Grants Economics* (Wadsworth, 1973), at p. 4 (according to Boulding, "the continuum for grants runs from gift, 'a grant made out of benevolence,' to tribute, 'a grant made out of fear and under threat'")).

342 *See* Ealy, *id.*, at p. 48 (citing Boulding, *The Economy of Love and Fear*, at p. 63).

343 *See Sweetened Charity*, THE ECONOMIST, June 9, 2012.

344 Paul Lewis, *Commitment, Identity, and Collective Intentionality: The Basis for Philanthropy*, 6 CONVERSATIONS ON PHILANTHROPY 47 (Donors Trust, 2009) (quoting Kenneth Boulding, "Notes on a Theory of Philanthropy," in F.R. Glahe, ed., *Collected Papers of Kenneth Boulding, Volume II* (Colorado Associated University Press, 1974), at 240).

virtue that could be promoted by legal provisions that encourage more direct and effective giving by Americans to foreign charitable causes.[345]

2.   Political Ideology and the Role of Philanthropy

In addition to individual donor motives, Americans' private philanthropy is impacted at home and abroad by political views regarding the appropriate extent of the government's role in providing social safety nets for its own citizens and international assistance to governments and individuals. The United States, of course, has long stood at the vanguard of private initiatives to solve societal problems. In one of the most famous passages in social science literature, de Tocqueville observed that

> Americans of all ages, conditions, and all dispositions constantly unite together. Not only do they have commercial and industrial associations to which all belong, but also a thousand other kinds ... Americans group together to hold fetes, found seminaries, build inns, construct churches, distribute books, dispatch missionaries to the antipodes. They establish hospitals, prisons, [and] schools by the same method. Finally, if they wish to highlight a truth or develop an opinion by the encouragement of a great example, they form an association. Where you see in France the government and in England a noble lord at the head of a great new initiative, in the United States you can count on finding an association.[346]

This historic preference for private solutions comprises an important aspect of the constant public discourse regarding the size and role of government in American society. Indeed, with respect to the persistent and growing federal budget deficit, while public discourse on the subject grows ever more rancorous, the foundational disagreements on government's role in areas from health care to education reflect certain shared assumptions and agreements, reflecting uniquely American values, on the limited nature of governmental responsibility and the importance of private initiatives.

Notwithstanding this baseline consensus on limited government, however, the functions of government over time have expanded beyond Americans' ability (or willingness) to pay for such government through taxes. At the federal level, the current budget deficit dilemma has been noted above in Chapter Two. In states and municipalities, the picture is no less grim, due in part to a deteriorating property tax base that reflects the growing role of nonprofit organizations in many cities and towns.[347]

---

345   *See* discussion *infra* in Chapter Six.

346   De Tocqueville, *supra* note 338, at p. 596.

347   *See. e.g.,* Susan Raymond, "The Tax Man Cometh: Should Nonprofits Pay?" in Raymond, Susan U., and Mary Beth Martin, eds., *Mapping the New World of American Philanthropy: Causes and Consequences of the Transfer of Wealth* (John Wiley & Sons, 2007), 251, 252-55 (discussing the "'nonprofitization' of local economies" and noting that in many cities, a large and growing percentage of land is exempt from property tax, *e.g.,* 74 percent of land in New Haven, Connecticut).

Accordingly, as the discussion in this book shifts to an exploration of the factors affecting international American philanthropy, it must be remembered that any discussion of expanded deductions must account for these sobering fiscal realities.[348]

II.   Moving Abroad: Ideology and Politics; Perceptions and Realities

1.   The Notion of the United States as the Most Generous Nation

Over the course of many years, and particularly during the latter half of the twentieth century – perhaps commencing in earnest with the United States' commitment through the Marshall Plan to rebuild Europe following the second World War – a broad consensus view has developed that Americans regularly lead the world in private philanthropic engagement on the international stage.[349] Indeed, certain empirical data would seem to underscore Americans' generosity abroad. With respect to developing country assistance, 2008 figures indicate that American individuals, private foundations, and corporations together gave over $49 billion, compared to $6.3 billion from United Kingdom sources and $1 billion from French sources.[350]

Other data, however, paint a less overwhelming portrait of private international charitable giving by Americans. Notwithstanding the relatively favorable tax treatment generally accorded to charitable contributions – described by two leading legal commentators as the most favorable in the world[351] – Americans concentrate the vast majority of their giving domestically. Keeping the balance of charity at home is to be expected, but the extent of the domestic share of private philanthropy may surprise many observers: a study published in 2006 suggested that only 2.5 percent of private charitable giving by Americans was devoted to international endeavors.[352] Further,

---

348   See Chapter Six for further discussion on this issue.

349   See, e.g., Advisory Committee on Tax Exempt and Government Entities, "Exempt Organizations: Recommendations to Improve the Tax Rules Governing International Grantmaking" (June 10, 2009), http://www.irs.gov/pub/irs-tege/tege_act_rpt8.pdf, at p. 3 (quoting comments in 2004 by Jonathan Fanton, then-president of the John D. and Catherine T. MacArthur Foundation, that "America has been the world leader in developing the independent sector at home and encouraging its growth abroad").

350   Charles R. Ostertag, We're Starting to Share Well with Others: Cross-Border Giving Lessons from the Court of Justice of the European Union, 20 Tul. J. Int'l & Comp. L. 255, 258 (citing Center for Global Prosperity, The Index of Global Philanthropy and Remittances 2010, Hudson Institute 12 (2010), http://www.hudson.org/files/pdf_upload/Index_of_Global_Philanthropy_and_Remittances_2010.pdf). Ostertag notes that American private philanthropy in 2008 to developing countries outpaced "official development aid" by the federal government by a nearly two-to-one ratio. See id. (citing Center for Global Prosperity data).

351   Victoria B. Bjorklund and Joanna Pressman, "Cross-Border Philanthropy," in Penina Kessler Lieber and Donald R. Levy, eds., Complete Guide to Nonprofit Organizations (Civic Research Institute, 2005), at p. 10-2. Nevertheless, such tax treatment, as explained in Chapter Three, is less favorable with respect to direct international giving by individuals, corporations, and even private foundations.

352   Susan Raymond, "It Really Is a Small World After All: Globalization and Philanthropy," in Raymond, Susan U., and Mary Beth Martin, eds., Mapping the New World of American Philanthropy: Causes and Consequences of the Transfer of Wealth (John Wiley & Sons, 2007), 49, 53 (citing Giving USA (Glenview, IL: Giving USA Foundation, 2006) ("Giving USA")). Raymond does, however, state that international giving had grown from 2 percent to 2.5 percent of total philanthropy during the decade to 2006 (citing

among private foundations, international giving is highly concentrated among a few large foundations.[353]

Moreover, in the crucial area of aid to developing countries, American charitable giving abroad – while still impressive – does not eclipse that from other peer rich nations. According to the Organization for Economic Cooperation and Development ("OECD"), in 2005-06 the average American contributed $30 per person to charities for expenditure on programs in poor countries – a number that indeed holds its own with, but hardly overwhelms, Dutch citizens' giving rate of $17 per person, and Germany's rate of $16 per capita.[354] Furthermore, when aid through public (government) funds is added to private philanthropy, the picture changes even further. In 2005-06, the combined flow of American tax dollars and private funds to developed countries was $115 per person ($85 from tax dollars). Germans, by comparison, gave $139 per person ($123 from tax dollars), while citizens of the United Kingdom gave $199 per person ($190 from tax dollars), Swedish citizens gave $398 per capita ($397 from public funds), and Norwegians an astounding $592, exclusively from tax dollars.[355]

Clearly, as noted earlier, ideological and political differences lead to vastly different views on the propriety of devoting public funds to foreign aid. Indeed, robust public debates focus not just on policy principles but also on the efficacy of public foreign aid.[356] Accordingly, many would minimize the significance of the combined

---

Giving USA).

353 See id. (citing H. Ruffin, The Globalization of American Philanthropy (Civil Society International and Duke University, October 31, 2003) (52 percent of all private foundation giving internationally is undertaken by ten foundations as of 2001, admittedly down from 71 percent a decade earlier).

354 Giles Bolton, Africa Doesn't Matter: How the West Has Failed the Poorest Continent and What We Can Do About It (Arcade, 2007), at p. 75 (citing OECD data). United Kingdom citizens contributed $9 per capita, compared to $2 per capita from Italian and Japanese citizens and $1 per capita from Swedes. Interestingly, even when comparing purely private giving data, the United States does not top the table: Australians clocked in at $31 per person and Canadians at $34 per person, while Irish citizens gave $82 per person in addition to $207 per capita from tax dollars (admittedly in a bygone era of robust Irish economic expansion).

355 Id. Not surprisingly, giving figures vary significantly from one analyst to the next. See, e.g., Ostertag, supra note 350, at 258, suggesting that combined private and public foreign aid to developing countries by Americans in 2008 totaled $76.1 billion, or approximately $253 per person for a population of 300 million (citing Center for Global Prosperity, The Index of Global Philanthropy and Remittances 2010, Hudson Institute 12 (2010) (available online at http://www.hudson.org/files/pdf_upload/Index_of_Global_Philanthropy_and_Remittances_2010.pdf)). The OECD figures, however, represent consistent methodology in measuring various countries' public and private giving.

356 See, e.g., the arguments posited in Dambisa Moyo, Dead Aid: Why Aid is Not Working and How There Is a Better Way Forward for Africa (Farrar, Straus and Giroux, 2009), at p. 47 ("[t]he evidence against aid is so strong and so compelling that even the [International Monetary Fund] – a leading provider of aid – has warned aid supporters about placing more hope in aid as an instrument of development than it is capable of delivering"). Ms. Moyo offers the interesting argument that a foreign government's mass purchase of mosquito nets, as part of a malaria eradication program, may in fact displace indigenous manufacturers and distributors of nets, thereby wreaking microeconomic havoc in the service of macroeconomic developmental goals. Id. at p. 44. While her observations offer helpful insight into the sometimes counterintuitive challenges of international economic development, they also highlight the sometimes conflicting goals of economic development and the relief of acute existential threats, such

public/private giving totals cited above, suggesting that the private sector represents the only appropriate source of charity abroad (either for development purposes or otherwise).[357]

Irrespective of one's philosophical disposition on the issue of private versus public funding of international aid, or the conclusions one draws from the data regarding the utility of public foreign aid, it is important to maintain an accurate perspective on the scope and composition of American cross-border philanthropy. As indicated by the data reviewed in this section, Americans' giving abroad is robust but hardly unique in its extent when compared to giving by other rich countries – particularly when private and public funds are aggregated for comparative purposes. And among private foundations, a key element of American international philanthropy, international giving constitutes a relatively small portion of overall giving, and relatively few foundations accomplish a significant slice of that foreign grant making. Calls for further stimulus of private foreign philanthropy by Americans appear more compelling when placed against the backdrop of these facts rather than against unsupported and arguably inflated popular perceptions of America as a peerless international philanthropic hegemon.

2.   Foreign Skepticism of American Nongovernmental Organizations

The final factor considered herein – although by no means the only other issue that affects international philanthropy by Americans – relates to the persistent mistrust among some foreign citizens and governments regarding the authenticity of the charitable interests pursued by American nongovernmental organizations ("NGOs," including charities, civil society groups, religious organizations, and many others) and their philanthropic supporters. Such views are particularly difficult to quantify and verify, but recent episodes documented in the mass media evince, albeit anecdotally, the skepticism that American charities and philanthropists continue to face in some quarters of the globe.

In February 2012, Egypt's transitional government launched criminal prosecutions against several American civil society organizations operating in Egypt, alleging that the groups (including Freedom House) had received foreign funds illegally and had failed to register with the Egyptian government.[358] Several weeks

---

as fatal disease, in the developing world.

357   From a purely philosophical perspective, it can be argued that in truly democratic countries, public funding of international aid programs represents an indirect use of private funds, because freely elected legislators who do not reflect the aggregate policy preferences of their constituents will subsequently suffer defeat at the ballot box, as citizens seek to implement their own views on the proper use of their tax dollars (including the use of fewer or more tax dollars, either generally or on specific programs).

358   David D. Kirkpatrick, Egypt Rejects Registration Bids from 8 U.S. Nonprofit Groups, NEW YORK TIMES (Apr. 23, 2012) (http://www.nytimes.com/2012/04/24/world/middleeast/egypt-rejects-registration-bids-from-8-us-nonprofits.html?_r=1).

later, the government rejected the registration applications of eight American charities, including the Carter Center for Human Rights and a religious charity called Coptic
Orphans, on the grounds that "their activities violate Egyptian sovereignty."[359]

In July 2012, a particularly ominous development surfaced in Russia, where
legislators from the governing United Russia party proposed a national law pursuant
to which Russian charitable organizations receiving funds from foreign sources (including not only foreign governments but individuals and other private philanthropic
sources) would be required to register as "foreign agents" and, if found to be involved
in any political activity (a seemingly inevitable conclusion), would be subjected to
annual audits and investigations without warning for "extremist speech."[360] One
Russian legislator stated that Russian citizens needed the proposed law "to be able to
distinguish between civic initiatives and 'the influence of foreign capital and foreign
ideas'," singling out foreign charities that monitor elections for special mention.[361]
Russia's lower legislative chamber, the Duma, quickly approved the bill by a margin of
374 to 3,[362] and the upper chamber followed suit promptly and overwhelmingly.[363]

Following the passage of this bill, on September 19, 2012, the Russian government ordered the United States Agency for International Development (USAID) to
discontinue its work in Russia by October 1, a date that fell less than two weeks before
the holding of local elections.[364] The new law, enforced by the Russian Ministry of
Justice, carries the potential for fines, forced dissolution of charities, and even im-
prisonment.[365]

---

359   *Egypt Denies Licenses for 8 U.S.-Based Nonprofits*, THE CHRONICLE OF PHILANTHROPY/PHILANTHROPY TODAY (Apr.
       24, 2012), http://philanthropy.com/blogs/philanthropytoday/egypt-denies-licenses-for-8-u-s-based-
       nonprofits/46777. The rejection of the Coptic Christian charity's application appears to reflect the
       religious complexities that inevitably affect American Christian organizations' efforts to engage in
       countries with majority non-Christian populations, whether or not the American charities conduct
       overtly religious activities or programs exclusively featuring objectives solely related to human
       development (*e.g.*, poverty or disease eradication, orphan and widow care, or disaster relief).

360   Ellen Barry, *Foreign-Funded Nonprofits in Russia Face New Hurdle*, NEW YORK TIMES (July 2, 2012)
       (http://www.nytimes.com/2012/07/03/world/europe/russia-introduces-law-limiting-aid-for-
       nonprofits.html).

361   *Id.*

362   David M. Herszenhorn and Andrew Roth, *Russian Law Would Place Tougher Restrictions on Nonprofits*,
       NEW YORK TIMES (July 13, 2012) (http://www.nytimes.com/2012/07/14/world/europe/russian-law-would-
       place-tougher-restrictions-on-nonprofits.html?pagewanted=all).

363   Ellen Barry, *Russian Legislators Approve Greater Government Control Over the Internet and Nonprofits*, NEW
       YORK TIMES (July 18, 2012) (http://www.nytimes.com/2012/07/19/world/europe/russian-parliament-
       approves-greater-government-control-over-the-internet-and-nonprofits.html) (reporting upper
       house's approval vote of 141 to 1).

364   The International Center for Not-for-Profit Law, *NGO Law Monitor: Russia*, http://www.icnl.org/
       research/monitor/russia.html (web site last visited on March 3, 2013).

365   Ellen Barry, *As 'Foreign Agent' Law Takes Effect in Russia, Human Rights Groups Vow to Defy It*, NEW YORK
       TIMES (Nov. 21, 2012) (http://www.nytimes.com/2012/11/22/world/europe/rights-groups-in-russia-
       reject-foreign-agent-label.html?_r=0).

These recent episodes suggest that private international philanthropic efforts by American individuals and organizations will not necessarily enjoy the presumption of altruism in the countries in which they seek to help effect change. Such cynicism among foreign nationals may reflect the actual or perceived historic use of philanthropic organizations to aid and abet the United States' foreign policy goals,[366] resulting in suspicions that private charitable organizations serve merely as proxies for the accomplishment of geopolitical objectives. In any event, individuals and organizations seeking to engage in philanthropy abroad must develop an appreciation for the variety of views held by foreign nationals on the true objectives of American charitable efforts, which range from uniform gratitude on the positive end to presumptive hostility on the other.

With this sobering reminder of the cultural hurdles that accompany Americans' international philanthropic efforts, the focus of this paper now turns to a call for the pursuit of such efforts abroad, by individual Americans as well as corporations and private foundations, with a particular focus on approaches to philanthropic engagement that emphasize empowerment of and leadership by foreign NGOs. These approaches contrast with traditional models that feature American givers, rather than foreign recipients, as the identifiers of programmatic goals and the selectors of operational methods. In Chapter Five, I survey some of the most compelling rationales for an increase in the level of philanthropic activity through a learning-driven model that emphasizes the primacy of foreign indigenous leadership. In Chapter Six, I then offer a concluding examination of several discrete legal reforms that could promote such developments in American international philanthropy.

---

366   *See, e.g.*, Nina J. Crimm, *Through a Post-September 11 Looking Glass: Assessing the Roles of Federal Tax Laws and Tax Policies Applicable to Global Philanthropy by Private Foundations and Their Donors*, 23 VA. TAX REV. 1, 8-9 (2003).

Chapter Five:

Policy Arguments for the Promotion of "Learning-Driven" International Engagement by American Philanthropists

As the twenty-first century progresses through the middle stages of its second decade, nations, regions, and humanity itself confront a staggering array of challenges featuring social, economic, and numerous other dimensions. The complexity and interconnectedness of those issues seem to multiply at an exponential rate. In this environment, the United States finds itself still leading in many respects but no longer unrivaled as a source of technical expertise, financial resources, security, and development aid, as exemplified by China's engagement in Africa and Latin America.

Moreover, in an era of increasingly overstretched federal budgets in the United States, public funds do not provide a default option for those seeking the involvement of the United States in global problem solving. Faced with these tests and limitations, American leaders recognize the unique and indispensable assets offered by the philanthropic sector on the world stage. As noted by former United States Secretary of State Hillary Clinton shortly after she assumed her official responsibilities in that office, "the problems we face today will not be solved by governments alone ... It will be in *partnerships with philanthropy*, with global business, *partnerships with civil society.*"[367]

Nevertheless, as American philanthropists seek to increase their quantitative level of engagement with international problem solving, they also must pay attention to the qualitative aspects of their efforts. As noted earlier, skepticism has increased regarding the true objectives of American philanthropy. Furthermore, even well-meaning philanthropy and charitable programming by Americans can inadvertently intensify problems in other countries due to paucities of cross-cultural understanding and objectives that reflect the primacy of the helper's motives and needs, rather than those of the purported recipient of charity.[368]

The focus of this book reflects my perspective that in defining its objectives and methodologies, American philanthropy generally should shift its *modus operandi* from efforts to "save" individuals, communities, and nations to a posture of learning about

---

367   Advisory Committee on Tax Exempt and Government Entities, "Exempt Organizations: Recommendations to Improve the Tax Rules Governing International Grantmaking" (June 10, 2009), http://www.irs.gov/ pub/irs-tege/tege_act_rpt8.pdf, at p. 1 (quoting Hillary R. Clinton U.S. Sec'y of State, Remarks before the Global Philanthropy Forum) (emphases added).

368   For an excellent analysis of these phenomena in the context of short-term religious missions work, *see* Steve Corbett and Brian Fikkert, *When Helping Hurts: Alleviating Poverty Without Hurting the Poor ... and Yourself* (Moody Publishers, 2009). As Corbett and Fikkert observe, "one of the biggest problems in many poverty-alleviation efforts is that their design and implementation exacerbates the poverty of being of the economically rich – their god-complexes – and the poverty of being of the economically poor – their feelings of inferiority and shame." *Id.* at p. 59.

and from foreign leaders in order to encourage the efforts of such leaders.[369] As exami-ned further in Chapter Six, such a change could be stimulated by a few well-placed reforms to the legal framework that both undergirds and circumscribes American cha-ritable giving in the international context. First, however, I wish to explore some of the most compelling rationales for promoting such a shift in emphasis to learning-driven philanthropy. Those arguments include the production of more effective results, the development of greater innovation and risk-taking among philanthropists and grant recipients, the encouragement of identification between donors and donees as an expression of their common human interests, the more nuanced projection and pro-tection of United States national interests in a global environment increasingly sus-picious of Americans' motives, and the relief of overstretched budgets in federal agencies and international organizations.

I.   Learning-Driven International Philanthropy Can Help Produce More Effective Results, Particularly in Addressing Problems of Systemic Poverty

Throughout the first decade of this century, and sparked in part by the high-profile involvement of celebrities like Bono, George Clooney and Angelina Jolie, the American public developed a heightened awareness of the problems associated with poverty in less developed countries. Such challenges include the prevalence of diseases such as HIV/AIDS, malaria and tuberculosis; food insecurity; the lack of clean water and its lethal consequences; educational deficiencies and disparities; systemic gender inequa-lity and the lack of economic opportunities for women in many societies; disputes over rights to land and natural resources among rival nations and between majority and minority ethnic groups; and many others.

As media attention on such issues increased, so did the apparent resolve of governments to address them, as expressed in initiatives such as the United Nations Millennium Development Goals and agreements among leaders of rich country groups like the G-8 to commit specific thresholds of national expenditures (expressed as a percentage of gross domestic product) to poverty relief efforts. Additionally, a body of literature – both academic offerings and those addressed to a more popular audience – proliferated and helped advance public discussions of whether and how to address the multifarious problems associated with global poverty. While Jeffrey Sachs contri-

---

369   See id. at p. 144 (recruiting materials for short term missions work, for example, should "[s]tay away from the 'go-help-and-save-them' message and use a 'go-as-a-learner' message"). This paradigm shift can be illustrated – albeit with sheepish reluctance – by my personal experience. Prior to my first trip to South Africa to observe the work of HIV/AIDS-focused NGOs, I learned that the orphanage at which our team would be staying was planning to build a soccer field. Upon receiving this news, I excitedly suggested to the South African-born executive director of the American organization with whom I would be traveling that we should purchase, transport, and donate to the orphanage a supply of soccer balls and uniforms. My grand plan was met with the polite and wise proposal that we might instead ask the directors of the orphanage whether they had any need for balls or uniforms. Both items, as it turns out, were in plentiful supply; what was needed most was funding to pay laborers to build the field!

buted perhaps the most-discussed work in the genre to date with *The End of Poverty*,[370] many others provided a rich tapestry of diverging views.

New York University economist William Easterly has written eloquently on the subject of Western – particularly American – efforts to alleviate poverty in the developing world. Easterly posits that many such efforts have borne little fruit, and he argues that these failures stem largely from the West's tendency to frame problems and solutions in its own terms, rather than looking to individuals and organizations in developing countries for the construction of questions and answers.[371] Easterly contrasts traditional Western prescribers of solutions, whom he labels "Planners," with "Searchers" who instead seek solutions from indigenous sources:

> A Planner thinks he already knows the answers; he thinks of poverty as a technical engineering problem that his answers will solve. A Searcher admits he doesn't know the answers in advance; he believes that poverty is a complicated tangle of political, social, historical, institutional, and technological factors. A Searcher hopes to find answers to individual problems only by trial and error experimentation. *A Planner believes outsiders know enough to impose solutions. A Searcher believes only insiders have enough knowledge to find solutions, and that most solutions must be homegrown.*[372]

Easterly's approach often is contrasted with that of Sachs; indeed, Easterly draws the distinction sharply.[373] But popular discussions and actions undertaken (and perhaps

---

370   Jeffrey D. Sachs, *The End of Poverty: Economic Possibilities for Our Time* (Penguin Books, 2006).

371   *See generally* William Easterly, *The White Man's Burden: Why the West's Efforts to Aid the Rest Have Done So Much Ill and So Little Good* (The Penguin Press, 2006).

372   *Id.* at 6 (emphasis added). Arguing that local problem-solving efforts in international development reveal a market-based approach that values flexibility and innovation, Easterly also writes that "[e]ven when the West fails to 'develop' the Rest [of the world], the Rest develops itself. The great bulk of development success in the Rest comes from self-reliant, exploratory efforts, and the borrowing of ideas, institutions, and technology from the West when it suits the Rest to do so." *Id.* at 363.

373   *See id.* at 6 (pejoratively describing Sachs's "intellectual solutions" as comprising a misguided top-down "Big Plan to end world poverty"). The fact that Sachs essentially advocates a massive increase of development aid without major systemic changes is criticized by Professor Frank Emmert, namely that "the continuation of development aid focused on the supply of 'schools, clinics, roads, electricity, ports, soil nutrients, clean drinking water, and the like' [Sachs, *supra* note 370, at 226] is a continuation of fifty wasted years, a continuation of construction without foundations, houses built on sand. Africa in particular is littered with so-called white elephants, grandiose projects like fertilizer factories, dams for electricity generation, ports, railroads, and so on, that are underperforming at best, mothballed at worst. The problem was and continues to be that these kind of projects are implemented solely with the upper class, the government and business elite, of the respective countries. Unfortunately, [...] the benefits so lavishly provided by the West rarely trickle down to the rest of the population." Emmert continues by observing that "Sachs argues for an increase of [official development aid] to somewhere between 135 and 195 billion US$ per year (from a current amount just above 100 billion US$), and claims that this would eliminate the worst forms of poverty – existence on less than 1 US$ a day – by the year 2025. However, Sachs does not even begin to provide the answers to the question how and why the additional money would not disappear just as the previous 6-8 trillion US$ [given in the last

prompted) by the academic debate between Easterly's and Sachs's respective approaches display an appreciation for the merits of both schools of thought. Many critiques of contemporary development efforts, whether through philanthropic support or programmatic engagement, seem to evince Sachs's sense of urgency in elevating the importance of development efforts while advocating a "bottom-up" approach that echoes Easterly's preference for "Searchers" over "Planners."

Consider, for example, the challenges associated with developing orphan drugs, *i.e.*, drugs for which a dearth of potential patients exists in rich-world markets. One economist criticizes the utility of corporate social responsibility programs designed to provide such drugs directly to afflicted individuals in sub-Saharan Africa:

> [Such programs assume] that the poor of Africa do not know their own best interests ... why isn't the solution [instead] to have U.S. corporations give money directly to the poor? That way the poor can chose how they want to spend their charity: on vaccines, or if they prefer, on cell phones, on food, or even on beer ... If ... the African poor have other priorities, then they will spend the money on something other than the vaccine, and be better off for it.[374]

Even proponents of solutions with Western origins emphasize the importance of sensitivity to local vagaries, which inevitably are illuminated most effectively by indigenous leaders and organizations.[375] Indeed, Bono – the celebrity who arguably thrust Sachs into the spotlight of broad public consciousness – sounds positively "Easterlian" as he makes the case for local leadership of international efforts to manage natural resources: "If I've learned anything in more than 25 years of making noise about [develop-

---

50 years] have disappeared without bringing about much development. His recipes are old school and bound to fail. Given the fact that *Sachs* already committed major blunders when pushing the Russian government under President Jelzin into 'shock therapy' for its economy and is – after Jelzin himself – probably the single most responsible person for the current inequality in the distribution of wealth in Russia, pretty much anything he says should be taken with a lot of care." Frank Emmert, Market Economy, Democracy, or Rule of Law? What Should Be Prioritized to Promote Development?, in Astrid Epiney, Marcel Haag and Andreas Heinemann eds., *Challenging Boundaries – Essays in Honor of Roland Bieber* (Nomos, 2007), pp. 104-116, at pp. 115-16.

374 Gregory Clark, "But Wait! Can't the Poor Decide for Themselves?," in Michael Kinsley and Conor Clarke, eds., *Creative Capitalism* (Simon & Schuster, 2008), at pp. 52-53. British economist Paul Ormerod also posits the superiority of the bottom-up approach in applying Hayekian analysis to international development, where "we make progress not by the 'rational' analysis of the central planner but by experiment and evolution," and in emphasizing that he is "particularly wary of the central-planning mentality that often goes with [corporate social responsibility]." Paul Ormerod, "Why Not Experiment?," in Kinsley and Clarke at pp. 126-27.

375 *See, e.g.*, Timothy Besley, Review Essay, *Poor Choices: Poverty from the Ground Level*, 91 Foreign Affairs 160, 162 (2012) (reviewing Abhijit V. Banerjee and Esther Duflo, *Poor Economics: A Radical Rethinking of the Way to Fight Global Poverty* (Public Affairs, 2011)) ("Banerjee and Duflo ... unapologetically propose a [poverty relief] solution they acknowledge to be paternalistic: outside interventions by those who know best. But ... Banerjee and Duflo are careful to tailor their recommendations to the circumstances on the ground.").

ment work], it's that partnership trumps paternalism … let's hope the G-8 and G-20 listen more intently to the people we hope to serve …."[376]

If Americans' international philanthropy were to reflect more of Easterly's preferred "searcher" approach rather than a "planner" mentality reflecting the assumption that Americans know best, grant makers could – and I would argue they should – achieve more effective results, as argued by the economists and others cited above. Furthermore, such a bottom-up posture of grant making, with an emphasis on learning on the part of grant makers, could help alter perceptions in some foreign countries of American philanthropists as condescending neo-colonialists who pursue U.S.-centric objectives and provide financial support only where such support aligns with predetermined grant program goals as defined by the American grant maker, rather than meeting the needs discerned by local leaders and organizations on the ground.

II.   Learning-Driven International Philanthropy Can Stimulate Greater Innovation in Development Efforts Among Charities

In addressing poverty-related problems in the developing world, public agencies and private grant makers alike understandably gravitate toward larger and more established organizations and programs. Such "known quantities" provide a greater measure of perceived certainty for funders in environments in which people, language, geography, history, laws, traditions, and other factors often are unfamiliar to grant makers. Much like investors in the stock market, many philanthropists find comfort in giving to established entities with mature track records and long histories of engagement in particular locales and/or program areas – particularly when large grant amounts are at stake.

Nevertheless, in the charitable world, including (but not limited to) the field of international development, bigger and older are not always synonymous with better. In some cases, intractable problems of poverty call for fresh thinking and risk taking, but large, established charities, governmental programs, and funders (including American philanthropists) may demonstrate institutionally risk-averse tendencies that hinder innovative problem-solving analysis and techniques. Oxford economist Paul Collier, in discussing efforts to address systemic problems in failed or failing states, observes as follows:

> Aid used … to support incipient turnarounds would be pretty high-risk … The process of aiding turnarounds is thus analogous, in terms of risk-taking, to a venture capital fund … The venture capital fund approach is, I think, the right managerial model for dealing with such risks because it reconciles accountability with incentives. A "venture aid fund" preserves

---

376   Bono, *The Resource Miracle*, TIME (May 28, 2012) (http://www.time.com/time/magazine/article/0,9171,2115044,00.html).

accountability for overall performance, but managers can achieve overall success despite a lot of failures. Without this sort of model bureaucracies just cannot cope with risk. Their staff will not take large risks because they imply periodic failure, and failure means a blighted career. Unsurprisingly, people are simply not prepared to take risks on these terms. The situation is getting worse as people are increasingly assessed in terms of the "results" they achieve. Within aid agencies there is a vogue for a results orientation, and up to a point this is sensible ... But a focus on results can very easily encourage people to avoid failures at all costs. And if this happens aid will increasingly be directed to the safe option of countries where performance is already satisfactory.[377]

Collier's observations at the macro-level of aid agencies addressing failing states also offer valuable insight at the micro-level of private philanthropies addressing international charitable efforts in the fields of health, human rights, education, and other aspects of human development. Laura Arrillaga-Andreessen, who founded the Silicon Valley Social Venture Fund and teaches philanthropy at Stanford University, describes philanthropy as "society's risk capital" carrying a corresponding mandate for innovation by grant makers and charitable managers.[378] Like many other entrepreneurs who apply lessons learned from venture capital-funded commercial endeavors to their philanthropic undertakings, Ms. Arrillaga-Andreessen emphasizes the importance of bringing "new thinking to old [societal] problems, processes and systems" in both domestic and international settings.[379]

But the focus on risk taking by philanthropists represents a relatively recent development in a field historically dominated by more conventional and "safe" modes of giving, particularly among many private foundations that collectively constitute a key pillar of private American charitable grant making. During the mid-1980s, Waldemar Nielsen noted that the areas in which private foundations focus "are on the whole traditional and noncontroversial; their preferred grantees are established ... institutions."[380] Nielsen added that "the great majority [of foundations] are not on the whole disposed to ... serve as catalysts of institutional or social change ... the profile of their activity is clearly conventional, not reformist. They are overwhelmingly institutions of social continuity, not change."[381]

---

377   Paul Collier, *The Bottom Billion: Why the Poorest Countries are Failing and What Can Be Done About It* (Oxford, 2007), at p. 117.

378   Rahim Kanani, *Laura Arrillaga-Andreessen on 21st Century Philanthropy and Smarter Giving*, FORBES (May 24, 2012), http://www.forbes.com/sites/rahimkanani/2012/05/24/laura-arrillaga-andreessen-on-21st-century-philanthropy-and-smarter-giving/. Arrillaga-Andreessen also leads a private foundation that bears both her name and that of her husband, the well-known software designer and entrepreneur Marc Andreessen.

379   *Id.*

380   Waldemar Nielsen, *The Golden Donors* (E.P. Dutton, 1985), at p. 423.

381   *Id.*

The traditional disposition of grant makers toward established recipients and programs may flow in part from the high level of legal regulation under which they labor, including the restrictions against various types of taxable expenditures, as discussed in Chapters Two and Three. Nielsen has noted, for example, the "paralyzing effect … on innovativeness" of the outright bans on political campaign activity and lobbying that apply to private foundations.[382] In the international context, commentators have noted that the lobbying restriction, which also applies to the undertaking or funding of efforts to change foreign laws, effectively stymies American grant makers from helping foreign charities to promote civil society reforms in their respective countries.[383]

In addition to the very real limitations imposed by the complex legal framework described in Chapters Two and Three, institutional aversions to risk taking among philanthropists may, of course, reflect other factors such as political climates or scientifically informed managerial views on the role and limits of experimentation.[384] Regardless of its genesis, however, any reflexive or categorical preference for the established over the new on the part of grant makers will lead to missed opportunities, particularly in the developing world. Jeffrey Sachs characterizes the "seed funding of solutions" and "social entrepreneurship and problem solving" as two of the "five key roles" of philanthropists and NGOs in "global problem solving."[385]

By spurring innovation among foreign NGOs, American private foundations – along with individuals, corporations, and internationally focused public charities – could forge new paths toward solutions to the most stubborn systemic problems prevalent in the developing world. Of course, not every aspect of international

---

382   Waldemar A. Nielsen, *The Big Foundations* (Columbia University Press, 1972), at p. 19. Nielsen also notes that the expenditure responsibility requirements imposed on certain grants under Code section 4945(d)(4) make it "extremely risky for a foundation to make a grant to other than a well-established institution." *Id.* at 20.

383   *See, e.g.,* Nina J. Crimm, *Democratization, Global Grant-Making, and the Internal Revenue Code Lobbying Restrictions*, 79 Tul. L. Rev. 587, 602-03 (2005) (positing that "without the tax constraints [on lobbying]," foundations could help "more foreign NGOs … to participate constructively in the transformation of their countries' laws and governmental policies").

384   *See, e.g.,* Nielsen, *The Big Foundations, supra* note 382, at p. 397 (private foundations' "inhibitions [also] are the product of an inhospitable political atmosphere which has led to self-restriction by foundations"), and Paul Ormerod, "Why Not Experiment?", in Michael Kinsley and Conor Clarke, eds., *Creative Capitalism* (Simon & Schuster, 2008), at pp. 126-27 (Hayek's views on experimentation should lead more philanthropists to "experiment and see what works").

385   Jeffrey D. Sachs, *Common Wealth: Economics for a Crowded Planet* (Penguin Books, 2008), at p. 291-92. The other roles identified by Sachs include "public advocacy," "accountability of government and the private sector," and "scientific research" by academics and others. *Id.* Notably, these passages actually demonstrate a keen sensitivity to the role of innovation and risk-taking by Sachs, whose approach to international development has been characterized (some might say caricatured) by Easterly and others as overly planned and top-down. *See also id.* at 304-05 (citing Muhammad Yunus and Grameen Bank as examples of the critical role played by "individual entrepreneurs" and "innovators" in "foster[ing] the multiplication of ideas" in international development that may be funded by philanthropists and government agencies).

development is well suited to intervention by private philanthropy; some problems present challenges of scale that can be confronted only by governments or international agencies (*e.g.*, the United Nations Development Programme or the International Committee of the Red Cross). Nevertheless, private philanthropy can play an effective role even in such large-scale contexts.[386]

In sum, American philanthropists seeking effective engagement in the developing world must be willing to pursue innovative efforts that carry risks of perceived failure. As the home of countless entrepreneurial success stories in wide-ranging fields such as agriculture, manufacturing, technology, and others, the United States should lead the world in bringing innovation to philanthropic problem solving on the world stage.

Nevertheless, temptations toward the conventional and the known persist among grant makers. Arguably, this phenomenon may demonstrate an overarching concern with strict compliance with legal rules governing the grant making enterprise, rather than the effecting of change, as the primary goal of philanthropy, that is, allowing the legal constructs that surround philanthropy to define what constitutes achieving a charitable goal. By empowering more local foreign charities to exercise greater degrees of control and freedom in identifying and pursuing solutions, a learning-driven approach to grant making could offer an antidote to some grant makers' excessive concentration on their own objectives, shifting their focus to a learning posture that seeks wisdom from prospective grantees on the areas of greatest need and the modes of assistance that would be most helpful.

III.   Learning-Driven International Philanthropy Can Allow Donors to Express a Key Motive for Charitable Giving by Enhancing Their Sense of Identification with Others

As noted in Chapter Four, one of the factors motivating charitable donors is the desire for identification or solidarity with others.[387] Economist Kenneth Boulding has written that "[o]ne of the most important aspects of the grants economy is the role it plays in the building up of integrative structures and communities – that is, groups of people

---

386   *Cf., e.g.,* Timothy Besley, Review Essay, *Poor Choices: Poverty from the Ground Level*, 91 FOREIGN AFFAIRS 160, 167 (2012) (success in smaller-scale projects (which may be implemented in the private sector as well as by government) may yield lessons for projects of greater scope), and *Spreading Gospels of Wealth*, THE ECONOMIST, May 19, 2012, at p. 36 (examining discussions among super-wealthy philanthropists such as Warren Buffet, Bill Gates, and others for the purpose of improving the effectiveness and transparency of their giving programs; such "mega-philanthropists," whose foundations' annual payout requirements are calculated in hundreds of millions of dollars, could impact charitable projects on scales approaching those that traditionally could be addressed only with government-sized resources).

387   *See* Paul Lewis, *Commitment, Identity, and Collective Intentionality: The Basis for Philanthropy*, 6 CONVERSATIONS ON PHILANTHROPY 47 (Donors Trust, 2009).

who have some feelings of identification and benevolence toward each other."[388] Others have built on Boulding's observation, reasoning that in his view of philanthropy, donors' desire for identification with the recipients of their charity reflects a societal preference for expressing norms in a collective, rather than purely personal, sense.[389] Commentators also have noted the centrality of learning to philanthropy in Boulding's view of philanthropy.[390]

Political scientists also have noted the role of identification in philanthropy as a means of strengthening societal bonds. In describing the "social capital" that binds citizens together more closely, Robert Putnam cites John Dewey's distinction between "[d]oing good *for* other people, however laudable," and "works of social connection – doing *with*."[391]

Personal religious motivations, of course, also can spur philanthropic engagement by facilitating identification between donors and recipients. While an exposition of the religious aspects of this dynamic exceeds the limitations of this book, it is worth noting that a sense of common identity with beneficiaries pervades multiple expressions of faith and motivates not only philanthropic giving but active charitable engagement.[392]

---

388   Kenneth Boulding, *The Economy of Love and Fear: A Preface to Grants Economics* (Wadsworth, 1973), at p. 27. Paul Lewis also notes Boulding's assertion that charitable giving actually helps construct the donor's identity by "identif[ying] the giver with the recipient." Lewis, *supra* note 387, at 56 (citing Boulding, *The Economy of Love and Fear*, at pp. 27-28).

389   Gordon Lloyd, *Boulding's Global-Socialist Theory of Philanthropy*, 4 CONVERSATIONS ON PHILANTHROPY 1 (Donors Trust, 2007), at p. 8 ("Boulding's general system of doing good looks at the [fulfillment] of the intentions of an entire 'value system' and not just … one person's values, regardless of whether we are talking about the preferences of the donor or the wishes of the recipient").

390   *See id.* at p. 9 ("the ethical principle underlying philanthropic conduct seems to be 'the principle of being willing to learn,' and the question undergirding the philanthropic project finally appears: 'How do we produce the will to learn?'").

391   Robert D. Putnam, *Bowling Alone: The Collapse and Revival of American Community* (Simon & Schuster, 2000), at pp. 116-17 (emphasis in original). Putnam thus describes charitable giving as a complement to, rather than a substitute for, active volunteerism. *Id.* at 118.

392   *See, e.g.,* Holy Bible (New Living Translation; Tyndale House Foundation, 2007) at Matthew 25:31-45 (Jesus explaining to his disciples that in feeding the hungry, displaying hospitality to strangers, providing clothing for the needy, caring for the sick, and visiting prisoners, it is as if they do such things for Jesus himself). An early bishop of Alexandria noted that second-century Christians identified uniquely with plague victims: "Heedless of the danger, they took charge of the sick, attending to their every need, and ministering to them in Christ. And with them [such Christians] departed this life serenely happy, for they were infected by others with the disease, drawing on themselves the sickness of their neighbors, and cheerfully accepting their pains." John Ortberg, *Who is This Man? The Unpredictable Impact of the Inescapable Jesus* (Zondervan, 2012) at p. 39 (quoting Dionysius, bishop of Alexandria, as cited by Rodney Stark, *The Rise of Christianity: How the Obscure, Marginal, Jesus Movement Became the Dominant Religious Force* (HarperOne, 1996), chapter 4). *See also* John L. Esposito, *Ten Things to Know About Islam* (Middle East Policy Council), http://www.teachmideast.org/essays/35-religion/58-ten-things-to-know-about-islam (describing the Islamic practices of zakat, which "is an obligation for those who have received their wealth from God to respond to the needs of less fortunate members of the community," and the fast of Ramadan, which promotes "identification with and response to the less fortunate"). *See also* William J. Jackson, *Seven Myths of Philanthropy; Seven Opportunities in Understanding*, 7 CONVERSATIONS ON PHILANTHROPY 25 (Donors Trust, 2010), at p. 36 (Buddhist values are

The objectives of community-building or "identification" between donors and donees clearly may be sought in local domestic contexts, *e.g.*, where wealthy donors seek commonality with less fortunate residents of the same municipality by giving to community development programs through United Way agencies or community chest vehicles. Additionally, however, writers have noted the prominence of identification as a motivation for charitable giving across national borders. Boulding, for one, has theorized that while foreign charitable assistance at its most base level can reflect "threat grants" designed to achieve political and diplomatic goals, "integrative" international grant making "represents an extension of the principle of 'commensality' to all mankind."[393]

One ironic manifestation of cross-border commonality examined by observers is the shared "poverty" between the materially wealthy and destitute. Earlier in this book, I alluded to Corbett and Fikkert's exposition of the notion of a common "poverty of being" of the rich (manifested in a messianic sense of indispensability to the poor through missions efforts) and the poor (evinced through "feelings of inferiority and shame").[394] Sociologist Robert Bellah concluded his classic work *Habits of the Heart* with a similar commentary on America in the closing decades of the twentieth century, which applies with equal force today:

> Above all, we will need to remember our poverty. We have been called a people of plenty, and though our per capita GNP has been surpassed by several other nations, we are still enormously affluent. Yet the truth of our condition is our poverty. We are finally defenseless on this earth. Our material belongings have not brought us happiness ... We have imagined ourselves a special creation, set apart from other humans... [but] we see that our poverty is as absolute as that of the poorest of nations. We have attempted to deny the human condition in our quest for power after power. *It would be well for us to rejoin the human race, to accept our essential poverty as a gift, and to share our material wealth with those in need.*[395]

Such notions of shared poverty can help transform perceptions of philanthropy as a sacrificial surrender of resources into an avenue for achieving goals that are as essential to the well-being of the giver as to that of the recipient. Nobel laureate Amartya Sen, in a discussion of international development economics, explains that

reflected when "the person with a fortune ... go[es] outside [the] profit system and add[s] philanthropy to his activities" as a means of expressing that "the other's well-being is not separate from our own").

393   Boulding, *The Economy of Love and Fear*, *supra* note 388, at 81 (also noting that an awareness of "the unity of mankind" has prompted increased levels of foreign assistance by national governments).

394   Steve Corbett and Brian Fikkert, *When Helping Hurts: Alleviating Poverty Without Hurting the Poor ... and Yourself* (Moody Publishers, 2009), at p. 59 (described in note 368).

395   Robert N. Bellah, et al., *Habits of the Heart: Individualism and Commitment in American Life* (Harper & Row, 1985), at pp. 295-96 (emphasis added).

arms' length philanthropy may not require any "sacrifice of self-interest" on the part of the giver, as "[h]elping a destitute [person] may make you better off if you suffer at his suffering."[396] Even "committed [charitable] behavior," according to Sen, if motivated not by the desire to relieve one's "sympathetic suffering" but by a "sense of injustice," still can promote self-interest through identification with the poor: "there is still an element of one's 'self' involved in the pursuit of one's commitments, since the commitments are one's own."[397]

Thus armed with the understanding that identification with the needy can motivate philanthropic engagement effectively, particularly in the developing-world setting, the power of the learning-driven model becomes ever more clear. If a giving program is undertaken based on goals predetermined by grant makers, and if grantees are entrusted with little more than the mandate to carry out such goals (perhaps through operational methods also determined in advance by grantors), then precious little identification between givers and recipients can be realized. Such a bifurcated model – featuring not only continued separation but *stratification*[398] between paternalistic donors and supplicant donees – is only exacerbated in the international arena. There, cultural, linguistic, historic, and political factors can combine to construct a narrative of condescension by rich-world patrons offering the poor "crumbs from their table"[399] at least in part to meet an individual donor's psychological needs or a country donor's strategic self-interest.

When private philanthropic efforts lack meaningful opportunities for decision-making by charitable recipients as to program objectives and operational choices, the stratification between rich and poor calcifies. On the other hand, a learning-driven model, in which donors seek first the wisdom and experience of those on the ground (*i.e.*, autochthonous leaders, not donor-country program directors living abroad), leads

---

396   Amartya Sen, *Development as Freedom* (Alfred A. Knopf, 1999), at p. 270.

397   *Id.* at pp. 270-71. Elsewhere, Sen has made a case for altruism as an expression of rational choice, even where individuals modify their own purely self-interested goals in order to pursue charitable commitments involving active engagement. Sen theorizes that such behavior does not violate "self-goal choice," as "[a]wareness and concern about other people's goals can lead to voluntary imposition of some constraints on one's own actions when others are involved, without that being interpretable as simply devoting oneself to the pursuit of 'other people's goals'"). Amartya Sen, "Rational Choice: Discipline, Brand Name, and Substance," in Fabienne Peter and H.B. Schmid, eds., *Rationality and Commitment*, 339, 355 (Oxford University Press, 2007).

398   Amartya Sen has used this term to describe needy individuals in certain societies in the developing world. *See, e.g.*, Sen, *Development as Freedom, supra* note 396, at p. 62 ("those who are persistently deprived; for example, the usual underdogs in *stratified* societies") (emphasis added). In my view, the term also aptly illustrates the divide between rich-world donors and developing-world recipients of charity.

399   *See* the song "Crumbs From Your Table," from U2's album *How to Dismantle an Atomic Bomb* (Universal Music Group, 2004), which ironically and devastatingly skewers self-serving forms of aid to the developing world with lyrics written from the perspective of a developing-world aid recipient who finds that the rich world's concern for his plight has subsided in the post-Cold War era (e.g., "I was there for you … [w]hen you needed my help[;] [w]ould you deny for others [w]hat you demand for yourself?").

naturally to communities of interest and perspective that produce a greater degree of identification between recipients and donors of charitable funds.[400]

As donors adjust their giving paradigms to take greater account of – indeed, to place primary emphasis on – donees' perspectives regarding the areas of greatest need and the most effective means of meeting those needs, charitable giving can be made more responsive. Moreover, such a perspective not only recognizes donors' inherent limitations in understanding the needs of grantees, but it also can promote the very capacity of individuals in developing contexts to make decisions that lead to greater degrees of development by widening the spectrum of alternative futures that they perceive as possible.

Noting the importance of this dynamic in development efforts, economist Amartya Sen observes the insufficiency of the traditional utilitarian analysis by explaining that "[t]he utility calculus can be deeply unfair to those who are persistently deprived," in the sense that "deprived people tend to come to terms with their deprivation because of the sheer necessity of survival, and they may, as a result … even adjust their desires and expectations to what they unambitiously see as feasible."[401] Thus, Sen posits that development efforts should "favor the creation of conditions in which people have real opportunities of judging the kind of lives they would like to lead … These considerations require a broader informational base, focusing particularly on people's capability to choose the lives they have reason to value."[402]

These perspectives therefore underscore the value of a learning-driven approach to philanthropy in producing a commonality or identification between donors and charitable recipients, particularly in the international context. In writing on the potency of "integrative power" to produce systemic change across divergent cultures, Kenneth Boulding offers this observation, which serves as a useful capstone for a discussion of the advantages of learning-driven philanthropy: "Underlying the structure of integrative power is a complex network of communication and learning. The extent and the power of this network [depend] a great deal on the development of what might be called a *'learning identity'* and a culture that puts a high value on learning."[403]

---

400   On the connection between learning through giving and identification with the less fortunate, *see* Jackson, *supra* note 392, at p. 35 ("Encountering other perspectives we may come to realize that we are heirs to wisdom worldwide"). Jackson explains that sacrificial giving can produce a sense of this solidarity of wisdom: "Troubles of forgetting the whole – whole community, long-term cycles, whole humanity – exist because getting a sense of wholes is often difficult. *Short-term self-interest is a convenient, natural myopia.* Understanding a larger whole gives more accurate grasps of reality, and hope." *Id.* (emphasis added).

401   Sen, *Development as Freedom, supra* note 396, at pp. 62-63.

402   *Id.* at p. 63.

403   Kenneth Boulding, *Three Faces of Power* (Sage Publications, 1989), at pp. 117-18 (emphasis added).

Such an identity between donors and beneficiaries is crucial to producing a sustainable path of change that does not lead to paternalism but rather develops a rich relationship between giver and recipient. Such a relationship promotes a shared perspective on needs and methods by first seeking the recipient's wisdom and challenging the donor to seek greater understanding of the recipient's context, culture, and calculus regarding his or her hierarchy of concerns. This mutuality of understanding, in turn, not only carries the capacity for meeting development needs more effectively but also enhances retention among donors. By seeking out and learning from grantees' perspectives, donors will be less likely to respond to needs with "one-off" or episodic check writing. Rather, by learning from and identifying with recipients, grant opportunities can produce long-term, relationally based connections among donors and beneficiaries, which should lead to more authentic communities of interest across cultures, ethnicities, socioeconomic classes, and nationalities.

IV.   Learning-Driven International Philanthropy Can Project the United States' National Interests While Reflecting Core American Values

International philanthropy – when based on a desire to learn from grantees' perspectives, and if undertaken to develop a commonality of interest between donors and recipients as described in the preceding section – can produce other salutary effects from a uniquely American perspective. First, such philanthropic efforts can project and protect American interests in ways that are inherently unavailable via state-driven methods focused on military, diplomatic, or trade channels.[404] Additionally, by elevating the preferences and viewpoints of nationals on the ground, American philanthropists demonstrate a commitment to the fundamental American values of personal freedom and free-market meritocracy.

With respect to the promotion of the national interests on the world stage through Americans' international philanthropy, it must first be emphasized that such interests do not equate to colonial-era expansionist or imperialist objectives.[405] Indeed, traditional cross-border philanthropy, featuring goals and methods pre-determined by

---

404   United States Secretary of State John Kerry articulated this view in February 2013, in one of his first official speeches after taking office: "Foreign assistance is not a giveaway. It's not charity. It is an investment in a strong America and a free world." Tom Curry, *Kerry: Foreign aid is in America's self-interest,* NBCNews.com (February 20, 2013) (http://nbcpolitics.nbcnews.com/_news/2013/02/20/1703-1977-kerry-foreign-aid-is-in-americas-self-interest?lite). Kerry also observed that voids created by the absence of foreign assistance combined with diplomatic efforts would "quickly be filled by those whose interests differ dramatically from ours. We learned that lesson in the deserts of Mali [in late 2012 and early 2013], in the mountains of Afghanistan in 2001, and in the tribal areas of Pakistan even today." *Id.*

405   Note, for example, Kenneth Boulding's observation that even where philanthropists pursue "commensality," as he terms the "unity of mankind," they often "mix[] in ... another principle that still has elements of the integrative or 'love' side of the spectrum but is mixed with threat and fear. This principle might be called 'expansionism,' and it has been a crucial element in the international system ... In nations, expansionism becomes imperialism." Kenneth Boulding, *The Economy of Love and Fear: A Preface to Grants Economics* (Wadsworth, 1973), at pp. 81-82.

donors and offered to prospective recipients on a take-it-or-leave-it basis, actually carries the potential to devolve into private sector imperialism. By contrast, learning-driven American philanthropy can accomplish objectives consistent with the national interest, and it can do so more nimbly than government bureaucracies while promoting a more benign vision of American involvement in a globalized world that could temper the presumptions of hostility and self-interest that greet American efforts in some foreign quarters.

As to the nimbleness or efficacy of philanthropic endeavors in promoting national interests, many observers have noted that NGOs enjoy natural advantages over governments in projecting power. Harvard political scientist Joseph Nye, for example, argues convincingly that information is central to this endeavor in the twenty-first century and that information is increasingly available to and usable by non-state actors:

> Information can often provide a key power resource, and more people have access to more information than ever before. What this means is that world politics will not be the sole province of governments ... Both individuals and private organizations, [including] NGOs ... are empowered to play direct roles in world politics. The spread of information means that power will be more widely distributed and informal networks will undercut the monopoly of traditional bureaucracy.[406]

In governmental contexts, Nye has developed the now well-known concept of "soft power," which he contrasts with "hard" power channels such as military interventions and trade sanctions.[407] Others have recently adapted the concept to the philanthropic world, contrasting the hard power of grants with the soft power of thought leadership and agenda setting by prioritizing areas of involvement (e.g., HIV/AIDS or food insecurity) and selecting recipient organizations.[408] More broadly, legal scholars have noted that philanthropy can project soft power in a national interest sense by enhancing global perceptions of the United States, which in turn can mitigate the country's national security concerns.[409]

---

406   See Joseph S. Nye, Jr., The Future of Power (Public Affairs, New York, 2011), at p. 110.

407   Id. at p. 224 (discussing the original application of the soft power theory to nation-states).

408   See, e.g., Sean Stannard-Stockton, Philanthropists' 'Soft Power' May Trump the Hard Pull of Purse Strings, THE CHRONICLE OF PHILANTHROPY (April 18, 2010), http://philanthropy.com/article/article-content/65080/ (cited in Nye, supra note 406, at p. 224) (noting that even relatively large grants given by the largest private foundations, such as the Bill & Melinda Gates Foundation, are "negligible" in the context of overall giving to specific causes, but emphasizing that the "reputations [of such foundations] for selecting effective grantees is a form of soft power that has the potential to persuade others to give to the organizations they support ... [they] have far more soft power at their disposal [than] the hard power represented by their grant-making budgets").

409   See, e.g., Charles R. Ostertag, We're Starting to Share Well with Others: Cross-Border Giving Lessons from the Court of Justice of the European Union, 20 TUL. J. INT'L & COMP. L. 255, 274 (2011) (citing Garry W. Jenkins, Soft Power, Strategic Security, and International Philanthropy, 85 N.C. L. REV. 773, 844-46 (2007)).

Philanthropists' ability to project American interests abroad may be enhanced where care is taken to distinguish the activities of private grant makers from the official actions and positions of the United States government. Private foundation officials acknowledged this notion as early as the mid-twentieth century and emphasized the dangers associated with maintaining relationships too closely with the governments of the United States or other countries in which activities are conducted with the support of foundation grants.[410] Some may take a more cynical view of such soft power wielded by private philanthropists, however, as evinced by Russia's recent enactment of a law that would require nonprofits accepting foreign assistance to register as "foreign agents."[411]

As American philanthropists pursue their own areas of interest internationally, they build "social capital," to use Robert Putnam's term, on behalf of the United States in global affairs, which in turn depends not only on activity by philanthropists but also on "key enabling structural conditions" that support philanthropic activity, such as the tax law features discussed at length in Chapters Two and Three. Such social capital includes the burnishing of the image of America and Americans abroad, and particularly in parts of the developing world where undemocratic dictators sometimes received support from the West, particularly during the Cold War era. More recent American efforts to elevate and promote democracy and the rule of law could be strengthened by the efforts of philanthropists in countries where such conditions are absent or nascent.[412]

Importantly for purposes of the projection of soft power in the service of the United States' national interests, learning-driven philanthropy offers a model of engagement conducive to the building of trust with foreign nationals. More traditional forms of international grant making, featuring top-down decision making by American philanthropists and relatively little consultation with foreign nationals, tend to reinforce global perceptions of American paternalism. Learning-driven philanthropy,

---

410   Waldemar A. Nielsen, *The Big Foundations* (Columbia University Press, 1972), pp. 394-95 (quoting "American Foundations and U.S. Public Diplomacy," presented to a subcommittee of the House Committee on Foreign Affairs, July 22, 1958, reprinted by the Ford Foundation). Here, Nielsen posits that it may be possible for philanthropy to engage in "value-free, nonpolitical activity in the [realm] of ... international affairs." *Id.* at 394-95.

411   *See* Ellen Barry, *Foreign-Funded Nonprofits in Russia Face New Hurdle*, NEW YORK TIMES (July 2, 2012) (http://www.nytimes.com/2012/07/03/world/europe/russia-introduces-law-limiting-aid-for-nonprofits.html) (noting a blog comment by Aleksandr Ridyakin, a Russian member of parliament, that "[t]he ultimate goal of funding nonprofit organizations, as a form of 'soft power,' is a colored revolution ... The United States is trying to affect Russian politics [through private philanthropy]").

412   As noted in section III(1)(e) of Chapter Two, such efforts conceivably could involve critiques of, or the support of efforts to change, foreign countries' laws, which under current United States law would constitute impermissible lobbying if undertaken by private foundations. At least one legal scholar has argued for the liberalization of the excise tax framework that essentially prohibits private foundation lobbying so that private foundations may support lobbying activities undertaken by foreign NGOs that are designed to promote democratization. *See* Nina J. Crimm, *Democratization, Global Grant-Making, and the Internal Revenue Code Lobbying Restrictions*, 79 TUL. L. REV. 587 (2005), at pp. 652-53.

by contrast, deflects more skeptical interpretations of American international philanthropy as "democracy by proxy" (viz. the recent Russian laws) by placing authentic trust in local leaders, rather than American grant makers, as the primary resource for identifying key challenges and the best means to address them.

Perhaps equally importantly, in addition to promoting United States interests abroad, learning-driven philanthropy in the international arena models two values cherished by Americans: personal freedom and free market competition. As to the first value, a bottom-up model, which favors the making of decisions at or near the locus of the challenge sought to be addressed, manifestly elevates individual freedom on the part of those whom philanthropists seek to help.[413] Particularly during an era in which American foreign policy makers claim to value the promotion of democratic reforms in traditionally authoritarian countries and regions, the learning-driven approach to international philanthropy would complement such proclamations.

The competitive characteristics of learning-driven philanthropy reflect another value traditionally embraced by Americans across the political spectrum: the superiority of the free market over a planned economy (both in normative terms and from an efficacy perspective) in determining winners and losers. As noted in section I of Chapter Five, the critique of a "Planner" mentality in international development constitutes the core of William Easterly's objections to traditional models of foreign aid. On this issue, Easterly observes that "[t]he world's poor do not have to wait passively for the West to save them (and they are not so waiting). The poor are their own best Searchers."[414]

Of course, markets do not ensure success on the part of each participant, but over time they tend to function as meritocracies, rewarding ingenuity, innovation, responsiveness, and efficiency. Similarly, although some efforts identified and led by local "searchers" (in Easterly's vernacular) certainly will fail,[415] American philanthropists can view international assistance as a marketplace in which experimentation and risk taking will, over time, allow grant makers to identify the best ideas and the most effective leaders with whom they can partner in future charitable endeavors.

---

413   It can, of course, be argued that a top-down approach, which features a greater role (or even sole discretion) for the grant maker in selecting objectives and methods, enhances personal freedom as well, i.e., the freedom of the grant maker. But to the extent that stereotypes exist and persist regarding the propensity of American philanthropists to engage in international affairs only when it furthers their own interests rather than the needs of foreign nationals, such a top-down approach could simply bolster such stereotypes.

414   William Easterly, The White Man's Burden: Why the West's Efforts to Aid the Rest Have Done So Much Ill and So Little Good (The Penguin Press, 2006), p. 27.

415   Easterly acknowledges this reality but reiterates the value of the marketplace approach. See id. ("Homegrown development does not always work, as the poverty and political chaos in various parts of the world shows. Yet even when national development fails, the poor are more resourceful than Planners give them credit for.").

The notion of philanthropy as a marketplace is not novel. Indeed, one leading practitioner in the field of tax-exempt law has observed that the very notion of tax exemption in American law rests primarily on the importance of the private sector's competition with the government in providing charitable services.[416] And competition represents a fundamental feature of the grant making process, to which any grant seeker can attest. Particularly in the international arena, such competitive values can be undergirded by the origination of ideas and the design of their implementation *in situ* rather than in the grant maker's office. Learning-driven philanthropy models this healthy approach.

V.   Learning-Driven International Philanthropy Can Help Relieve the Burdens of Overextended Federal Agencies and International Organizations

Finally, the promotion of increased American engagement in international philanthropy also can play a role in relieving the ever increasing fiscal burdens of government agencies responsible for foreign aid and international organizations.[417] The extent to which the United States government is committed to foreign aid, while subject to exaggeration,[418] has risen dramatically in the years since Congress expressed its now-outdated sense that "[t]he United States derives no ... benefit from gifts to foreign institutions."[419]

Philanthropy and government naturally overlap in addressing charitable goals. Indeed, both charitable organizations and government agencies provide a solution to the failure of private, for-profit markets to meet charitable needs effectively.[420] Shortly after the passage of the seminal Tax Reform Act of 1969, Waldemar Nielsen observed that "all the fields in which [private] foundations operate are now also occupied by government ... Government in this sense has become a giant foundation – or an

---

416   *See* Bruce R. Hopkins, *The Law of Tax-Exempt Organizations* (10th ed., John Wiley & Sons 2011), at pp. 11, *et seq.* Hopkins notes that this value of the "pluralism of institutions ... between the nonprofit and government sectors" rests, in turn, on the "distrust of government." *Id.* at p. 11.

417   Such results admittedly could be achieved by promoting increased international philanthropy generally, rather than learning-driven philanthropy specifically. Nevertheless, some of the potential legal reforms that could promote more and better international grant making, which are discussed in detail in Chapter Six, would specifically encourage the learning-driven approach described above by encouraging greater and more direct international philanthropic engagement by individuals and corporations.

418   *See, e.g.,* the discussion in section II(1) of Chapter Four regarding the diminished standing of rates of American foreign aid to developing countries, relative to other donor nations, when private and public sources of aid are aggregated.

419   H.R. Rep. No. 1860, 75th Cong., 3d Sess. 19-20 (1938).

420   *See* Henry Hansmann, *The Rationale for Exempting Nonprofit Organizations From Corporate Income Taxation*, 91 YALE L.J. 54, 67-68 and 74 (1981), regarding the discussion of "contract failure" in private markets for charitable services as a rationale for offering tax exemption to organizations engaged exclusively in charitable activities.

aggregation of public foundations – working side by side with the private variety."[421] It is precisely this overlap that accounts for one of the definitions of the term "charitable" in the United States Treasury Regulations: "lessening of the burdens of Government."[422]

As noted in section III(5)(e) of Chapter Two, the fiscal challenges currently faced by the federal government arguably are unprecedented. Accordingly, federal agencies face real limits on their ability to meet challenges in many areas of government activity, including international development and other aspects of foreign aid. Private philanthropy cannot, of course, offer a complete stopgap.[423] Nevertheless, by encouraging more private involvement in international philanthropy via strategic legal reforms, government could bolster the sustainability of charitable endeavors in foreign countries by decreasing the dependence of foreign aid recipients on government funding sources that may diminish in the future.

Additionally, in purely quantitative terms, increased international philanthropic activity could mitigate (however marginally) the public fiscal challenge in the United States by reducing the need for certain government expenditures on foreign aid. If, as proposed in Chapter Six, international philanthropy is encouraged via the allowance of partial or total deductibility for individual or corporate gifts to foreign charities, liberalized deductibility could diminish federal revenues by decreasing the tax base. Nevertheless, to the extent that increased private charitable giving displaces (or replaces) federal spending, the government's net income still would increase, as the deductions would only reduce tax revenues by a fraction of each charitable dollar (*i.e.*, the percentage represented by a donor's marginal tax rate), while government spending would be reduced by the entire dollar.[424]

---

421 Waldemar A. Nielsen, *The Big Foundations* (Columbia University Press, 1972), at p. 380. Jeffrey Sachs recently observed that his academic training under Harvard economist Paul Samuelson featured the "core idea" that "[m]arkets systematically underprovide certain 'public goods,' such as infrastructure, environmental regulation, education, and scientific research, whose adequate supply depends on the government." Jeffrey D. Sachs, *The Price of Civilization: Reawakening American Virtue and Prosperity* (Random House, 2011), at p. 28. While the notion of under-delivery of public goods by private markets is undisputed, Sachs (at least in this context) fails to account for the role of nonprofit, tax-exempt organizations – subsidized by philanthropy – to provide certain public goods, *e.g.*, education. Government does not offer the only solution to the public goods dilemma.

422 Treas. Reg. sec. 1.501(c)(3)-1(d)(2).

423 *See* Waldemar Nielsen, *The Golden Donors* (E.P. Dutton, 1985), at p. 439, articulating this timeless dilemma in an earlier era ("[private foundations] cannot of course seek to replace the losses in government funding [due to decreases in federal expenditures], the disproportion between [foundations'] resources and [charities'] requirements being too extreme").

424 For example, Nina Crimm supports her argument for allowing grant makers to support lobbying in foreign countries by positing that such grants could result in "the burden of the duty to assist peacefully 'burdened societies' [being] shifted by the U.S. government to domestic grant-making section 501(c)(3) organizations." Nina J. Crimm, *Democratization, Global Grant-Making, and the Internal Revenue Code Lobbying Restrictions*, 79 Tul. L. Rev. 587, 662 (2005).

With respect to international organizations, the global economic slowdown of the past several years has negatively impacted their financial support and consequently has reduced their ability to address large-scale problems of poverty, disease, education, and other systemic deficiencies. For example, the current European financial crisis and other public economic challenges appear to have caused many developed Western countries to reduce their funding for the Global Fund to Fight AIDS, Tuberculosis, and Malaria (the "Global Fund"), which in turn recently announced the suspension of new grant making.[425]

The encouragement of more direct international engagement by individual and corporate American philanthropy could alleviate a measure of the revenue shortfalls currently experienced by the Global Fund and others, and it also could mitigate the fiscal challenges faced by one of the Global Fund's chief donors, the United States government. As noted above, such increased engagement through a learning-driven philanthropic model also could generate more effective problem solving in international development, spur greater innovation and risk taking by charities in their approaches to poverty and other systemic development issues, fulfill a primary motivation of charitable donors by allowing them to deepen and broaden their identification and solidarity with grantees, and promote the interests of the United States through the projection of soft forms of national power by nongovernmental actors.

In short, greater levels of learning-driven philanthropy by Americans on the international stage will benefit each of the players involved in American international development efforts: private and government recipients of charitable assistance in other countries, the United States government, and private donors themselves. But such benefits cannot be realized without aggressively challenging the status quo in international giving patterns. Several discrete reforms to the federal laws impacting international philanthropy could offer meaningful catalysts toward such changes. This book concludes with an examination of two such proposed reforms: the creation of a system for providing official sanctioning of repositories for equivalency determinations by private foundations, and the limited allowance of deductions from taxable income for individual and corporate charitable gifts made directly to certain foreign charities.

---

425   *See Downturn Forces Disease Fund to Suspend New Grants*, THE CHRONICLE OF PHILANTHROPY/PHILANTHROPY TODAY (Nov. 28, 2011), http://philanthropy.com/blogs/philanthropytoday/downturn-forces-disease-fund-to-suspend-new-grants/42390. Italy and Spain, two poster children of the Euro crisis, offer two egregious examples of nonperformance on recent pledges to the Global Fund and reductions in pledges of future support. *See Fund Halts New Grants for AIDS, TB and Malaria Treatment in Poor Countries*, WASHINGTON POST (Nov. 23, 2011), http://www.washingtonpost.com/national/health-science/fund-halts-new-grants-for-aids-tb-and-malaria-treatment-in-poor-countries/2011/11/23/gIQAPZdspN_story.html.

Chapter Six:

Legal Reforms to Encourage Learning-Driven International Philanthropy by Americans

While the general American legal framework governing domestic philanthropy offers a carefully designed and reasonable balance between encouragement and regulation, that balance is less evident in the context of internationally directed philanthropy. With respect to laws specifically affecting charitable giving by American individuals or entities in support of charitable endeavors outside the United States, such provisions tilt heavily in favor of regulation and away from encouragement. This asymmetry is evident in IRS pronouncements that amplify the application of the private foundation taxable expenditure rules in international grant making.[426] The enforcement-oriented nature of the legal framework also is manifest, perhaps most starkly, in the general disallowance of deductions from taxable income for charitable gifts made by individuals and corporations directly to foreign charities rather than through American intermediaries.[427]

The desire for caution is understandable in the laws affecting international philanthropy. Legal systems in many other countries have not developed to the same degree in their governance of philanthropy and charitable activity, making it difficult to discern whether certain organizations are "charitable" in the sense of that term as reflected in American law. Accordingly, it would be imprudent to permit unfettered private foundation grant making to foreign charities or unlimited tax deductibility for individual and corporate gifts to foreign charities. Furthermore, from a policy perspective, if charitable giving carries zero-sum characteristics for donors, then increased international philanthropy could reduce financial support for domestic charitable causes. Although such a potential phenomenon is difficult to predict or quantify, any proposal to liberalize deductibility for international gifts must address the visceral impact of its potentially adverse impact on domestic charities.

Care must be taken in offering new structures and instruments to stimulate charitable activity, whether domestically or internationally. The philanthropic field is relatively mature, as are the laws that have developed over time to govern philanthropic activity. Certain newfangled proposals initially purporting to resolve long-standing dilemmas eventually have been revealed as superfluous solutions to nonexistent problems, as is arguably true of recently adopted state-level legislative measures recognizing a new form of entity called the low-profit limited liability company ("L3C").[428]

---

426   See, e.g., Rev. Proc. 92-94, 1992-1 C.B. 507.

427   See Code section 170(c)(2)(A), discussed in section I of Chapter Three.

428   See William J. Callison and Allan W. Vestal, The L3C Illusion: Why Low-Profit Limited Liability Companies Will Not Stimulate Socially Optimal Private Foundation Investment in Entrepreneurial Ventures, 35 VERMONT L. REV. 273, 292-93 (critiquing the L3C model as a "sleight of hand" that reflects an improper

Additionally, the public policies supporting existing limitations or restrictions may offer compelling rationales for maintaining the status quo with respect to the legal framework for philanthropy, *e.g.*, concerns regarding the diversion of financial support away from domestic charities that potentially could result from the allowance of deductibility in connection with individual and corporate charitable gifts to foreign organizations. And finally, new legal approaches may feature technical challenges associated with implementation or cost, any or all of which could render them less workable in practice.

Nevertheless, while these technical and practical concerns are legitimate, they do not present insuperable obstacles to the encouragement of more – and more effective – international philanthropic activity by American donors through legal reform. Such reform could be effected through discrete and limited measures that account for the need to verify the legitimacy of charitable activities supported by international gifts and grants, the limited ability of the federal government to provide effective oversight and regulation of increased international philanthropy in light of current fiscal realities, and the potential drain on domestic charities' revenues – as well as tax revenues – that may result from increased tax-free international giving.

In this concluding chapter, I propose two specific reforms: (i) the implementation of a system for granting legal recognition to, and regulating, electronic databases or repositories of equivalency determinations for foreign charities, which could be used by private foundations to ensure that they avoid taxable expenditures in connection with grants to such charities and to ensure that such grants constitute qualifying distributions for purposes of foundations' minimum payout requirements; and (ii) the limited allowance of deductions under federal tax law for charitable gifts made by individuals and corporations directly to certain foreign charities, whose eligibility to receive tax-deductible gifts could be verified in part by utilizing the aforementioned repositories.

I.   Private Foundations, International Grant Making, and the Implementation of an Officially Sanctioned Repository for Equivalency Determinations

American private foundations seeking to engage in international grant making activity must address two primary limitations under federal tax law: the requirement to expend a certain amount each year on "qualifying distributions" that are carefully defined under Code section 4942, and the prohibition on taxable expenditures in the form of grants to non-qualifying organizations or for non-charitable purposes, as set forth in Code section 4945(d)(4) and (5).[429] In light of these rules, private foundations

---

understanding of the federal tax law rules on program-related investments ("PRIs") by private foundations, and positing that existing entity models likely offer more suitable vehicles for "encouraging and obtaining PRI investment in socially-beneficial enterprises").

429   *See generally* discussion in Chapter Three.

considering grants to foreign charitable organizations generally will undertake an equivalency determination process[430] or fulfill the expenditure responsibility require-ments prescribed by Code section 4945(h).[431]

Equivalency determinations offer certainty to private foundations seeking to engage in foreign grant making. Nevertheless, the equivalency determination process presents challenges for the would-be grant maker and the grant recipient. The fundamental burden in this regard is associated with the nature of the "currently qualified affidavit" required for the making of "reasonable judgments" regarding 501(c)(3) equivalency and "good faith determinations" of public charity equivalency under Rev. Proc. 92-94.[432] Such affidavits must be prepared in the English language, and they must include current financial or other data.[433] Both requirements often present high hurdles of compliance for foreign grant seekers and grant makers alike.[434] Likewise, private foundations may be deterred from foreign grant making by the numerous content requirements associated with equivalency determinations. Legal scholar Nina Crimm explains the burden on foundations as follows:

> Congress ... has done little to encourage domestic private foundations to make direct grants overseas, even though it might have done so in 1969 when it debated and passed the laws that govern those organi-zations. For example, a foundation that wants to provide direct support to a charitable organization abroad must figure out whether the grant recipient meets the same standards that the Internal Revenue Service uses to determine whether an American organization qualifies as a chari-ty for tax-exempt status under Section 501(c)(3) of the Internal Revenue Code. *A foundation that doesn't want to undertake the costly and time-consuming process of operating like a small-scale IRS* has an alternative [i.e., expenditure responsibility], but it is also complex, time-consuming, and problematic for most private foundations.[435]

---

430   *See* Rev. Proc. 92-94, 1992-1 C.B. 507.

431   Recall that fulfillment of the expenditure responsibility procedures will ensure avoidance of a taxable expenditure but not necessarily the treatment of a grant as a qualifying distribution. *See supra* note 277.

432   *See* Rev. Proc. 92-94, sec. 4.01.

433   Rev. Proc. secs. 5.01, 4.03, and 4.04. *See also* Bruce R. Hopkins, *The Tax Law of Charitable Giving*, 4th ed. (John Wiley & Sons, 2010), at p. 629 (explaining how affidavits may be made current where a foreign grantee's public charity equivalency does not depend on its ability to satisfy a public support test).

434   Nina J. Crimm, *Through a Post-September 11 Looking Glass: Assessing the Roles of Federal Tax Laws and Tax Policies Applicable to Global Philanthropy by Private Foundations and Their Donors*, 23 VA. TAX REV. 1, 128-29 (2003) (private foundation grant makers, when surveyed, "consistently labeled as a 'cumbersome ordeal' the process of obtaining English translations of the affidavit and other documentation required" and "commented that translations must often be repeated to assure accuracy, thereby resulting in additional cost").

435   Nina J. Crimm, *Global Philanthropy Depends on Tax Laws*, THE CHRONICLE OF PHILANTHROPY (Apr. 3, 2003), http://philanthropy.com/article/Global-Philanthropy-Depends-on/49750/ (emphasis added).

The notion of "operating like a small-scale IRS" is sufficient to deter many well-meaning private foundations (particularly small organizations with limited or no staff) from international grant making, instead encouraging them down the more familiar, relatively less burdensome path of making grants to domestic public charities. Even where such charities serve as intermediaries for the support of charitable activity in other countries, the net result is that American engagement in international philanthropy is conducted on terms set by American grant makers, for purposes established by American grant makers. This state of affairs perpetuates the traditional American-centric approach rather the learning-driven model focused on the empowerment of indigenous leadership and decision making.

1.   Existing Proposals for Centralized Repositories of Equivalency Determinations

In light of these burdens of compliance, philanthropic organizations and legal practitioners have called for the development of techniques that would streamline, routinize, and centralize the equivalency determination process for grant makers and foreign grant seekers alike. In particular, the Advisory Committee on Tax Exempt and Government Entities (the "ACT," an officially sanctioned body of citizen advisors to the IRS) has called for the IRS to "facilitate formation" of equivalency determination information repositories ("EDIRs") on which private foundations could rely in connection with their undertaking of the procedures prescribed in Rev. Proc. 92-94.[436]

Although the ACT offered its recommendation on EDIRs over three years ago, the IRS has not yet taken any action to "facilitate" their creation. The ACT specifically requested that the IRS issue a revenue procedure describing a template EDIR that would ensure consistency with the content and timeliness requirements of the equivalency determination provisions of Rev. Proc. 92-94.[437] Presumably, under such an approach, a private foundation donor utilizing an EDIR consistent with the features of the template described in the requested revenue procedure could rely on its use of that EDIR for purposes of ensuring the inclusion of its grant to a foreign charity as a qualifying distribution for purposes of Code section 4942 and avoiding taxable expenditure treatment for the grant under Code sections 4945(d)(4) and (5).

More recently, a group of private foundations and other grant makers echoed the ACT's 2009 recommendation by calling for amendments to Rev. Proc. 92-94 that

---

436   Advisory Committee on Tax Exempt and Government Entities, "Exempt Organizations: Recommendations to Improve the Tax Rules Governing International Grantmaking" (June 10, 2009), http://www.irs.gov/pub/ irs-tege/tege_act_rpt8.pdf, at p. 11. The ACT's report stated that officially sanctioned EDIRs would reduce the cost associated with equivalency determinations and could improve the consistency and quality of such determinations. *Id.* at pp. 12-13. According to the ACT, an overwhelming majority of private foundations surveyed (86 percent) indicated that such EDIRs would "benefit" American-based international philanthropy, and nearly all foreign NGOs surveyed (98 percent) indicated that they would submit their data to such EDIRs and would update the accuracy of that data. *Id.* at p. 14.

437   *See id.* at p. 14.

would recognize an official role for EDIRs in the equivalency determination process. In April 2012 letters to the IRS, the Grants Managers Network, the Rockefeller Foundation, the Michael and Susan Dell Foundation, Independent Sector, and others asked the IRS to grant an application for a private letter ruling submitted in 2009 by TechSoup Global, a would-be developer and operator of EDIRs, and a 2009 request from the Council on Foundations for a revenue procedure on EDIRs similar to that contempla-ted in the ACT's recommendation.[438]

2.   A Critical Response to Existing EDIR Proposals

Officially sanctioned EDIRs indeed would create uniformity in equivalency determi-nations while simplifying the process by standardizing the formats for providing and updating the information requested by private foundations pursuant to Rev. Proc. 92-94. Recent improvements in information technology and global digital communica-tions make the development and widespread use of EDIRs eminently feasible, and it is past time that EDIRs be recognized as an acceptable method for private foundations to fulfill the legal requirements associated with equivalency determinations.

Nevertheless, the efficacy of EDIRs in addressing the problems of cost and complexity will depend not just on *whether* they are officially recognized, but also on *how* that recognition is granted. In this regard, the recommendations of the ACT and the Grants Managers Network offer an appropriate substantive solution, *i.e.*, the use of officially recognized EDIRs. By calling for private letter rulings and/or revenue proce-dures to describe acceptable EDIRs, however, those recommendations may not offer the most efficacious methodological solution for the official recognition of EDIRs.

The IRS issues private letter rulings to taxpayers who seek certainty regarding the tax law consequences of specific proposed transactions or other courses of action. By definition, however, a private letter ruling is binding only as between the IRS and the particular taxpayer who sought the ruling, and it does not constitute precedential authority on which any other taxpayer may rely.[439] Accordingly, private letter rulings do not constitute a particularly effective means of establishing broadly applicable regimes or frameworks designed to provide assurances regarding the propriety of certain methods used to comply with legal requirements. This is no less true of the proposed use of EDIRs: even if the IRS were to approve TechSoup Global's proposal, the effect of a private letter ruling issued to TechSoup Global would be limited, at best,

---

438   *See* Diane Freda, *Private Foundations Ask IRS to Allow Repository for Foreign Grant Information*, BLOOMBERG BNA DAILY TAX REPORT, May 2, 2012.

439   Internal Revenue Service, *Understanding IRS Guidance – A Brief Primer*, http://www.irs.gov/uac/Under-standing-IRS-Guidance---A-Brief-Primer (web site last visited on March 3, 2013). While private letter rulings may not be cited by other taxpayers as precedential authority, they can illuminate the positions taken and rationales articulated by the IRS when confronted with particular legal issues under specific facts and circumstances.

to those private foundations who use the particular EDIR designed and maintained by TechSoup Global.[440]

Admittedly, there is nothing deficient about the adoption of public positions, whether by the Grants Managers Network or others, in support of TechSoup Global's private letter ruling request. Once such a request has been submitted, a favorable ruling certainly would constitute a preferable outcome (compared to a denial) for those favoring the official recognition of EDIRs. Nevertheless, the issuance of a favorable ruling to one private party would represent only a step in the right direction rather than a general solution. In this context, the revenue procedure approach suggested by the ACT represents a further, but not final, step in the right direction.

A revenue procedure, unlike a private letter ruling, is by its nature binding on the general taxpaying public, because it is designed to communicate "an official statement of a procedure that affects the rights or duties of taxpayers or other members of the public under the Internal Revenue Code, related statutes, tax treaties and regulations and that should be a matter of public knowledge."[441] Typically, a revenue procedure describes a hypothetical scenario and offers a template or sample framework for addressing the issues presented by that scenario in a manner that will allow taxpayers to avoid adverse tax law consequences.[442] Crucially, therefore, the facts confronted by the taxpayer must be sufficiently consistent with those described in the revenue procedure, and the means used by the taxpayer must be sufficiently aligned with those prescribed by the revenue procedure, for the taxpayer to rely on the legal conclusions reached therein.

From a regulatory perspective, a revenue procedure allows the regulator (the IRS) to offer broadly binding guidance to taxpayers in an efficient fashion and without the need to address specific individual requests that could overwhelm the regulator's available staffing resources. Accordingly, revenue procedures often represent a sensible approach to emerging tax law issues that reflect new developments in the field. On the other hand, revenue procedures are inherently limited by the fact that they seek to describe scenarios that may or may not precisely mirror the actual facts confronting a particular taxpayer. Individuals or organizations thus may be uncertain as to whether their situations are appropriately covered by a revenue procedure. As a consequence, some perfectly legitimate courses of action may be declined by overly cautious taxpayers, while other proposals may be pursued despite the fact that they

---

440   The utility of the private letter ruling conceivably may not expand even to private foundation users of TechSoup Global's EDIR, because TechSoup Global – not the potential private foundation users of the EDIR – is the taxpayer seeking the ruling. This technical distinction may or may not be at least partly responsible for the IRS's delay in ruling on TechSoup Global's request, but it does present a potential difficulty.

441   Internal Revenue Service, "Understanding IRS Guidance – A Brief Primer," *supra* note 439. In light of their broad applicability, revenue procedures are published in the Internal Revenue Bulletin. *Id.*

442   *See, e.g.,* Rev. Proc. 92-94.

do not comport with the requirements and safeguards contemplated by the IRS in a revenue procedure directed to a slightly different fact pattern. In the former scenario, the utility of tax law suffers, while in the latter, the integrity of tax law is compromised.

As applied to the EDIR question, the revenue procedure approach clearly represents a model more suited to broad applicability than a multiplicity of private letter rulings submitted by individual taxpayers, each of which could present a unique set of facts,[443] and which together do not offer a coherent framework for describing compliant repositories of information for purposes of satisfying the established requirements for equivalency determinations. Nevertheless, a revenue procedure has its own limitations, as it offers to taxpayers not a direct answer to a specific question, but only an ideal pattern to follow. This approach, while less burdensome to the IRS, leaves open the possibility of uncertainty on the part of a taxpayer as to whether a particular course of action (in this case, a specifically designed and implemented EDIR) sufficiently approximates the model or template described in the revenue procedure.

3.   Potential Paths for EDIRs Going Forward – and Avoiding Pitfalls Along the Way

Private foundations could obtain even greater levels of certainty regarding their equivalency determinations if specific EDIRs – or designers/operators of EDIRs – were to be individually certified or approved by the IRS. Under this approach, aspiring developers of EDIRs such as TechSoup Global could submit an application (not a request for a private letter ruling) to the IRS for approval of a proposed EDIR, described with specificity, and any EDIR receiving approval by the IRS could be used by any private foundation to rely on the sufficiency of its equivalency determination procedures for purposes of the qualifying distribution rules under Code section 4942 and the taxable expenditure rules under Code section 4945(d)(4) and (5).

The application process and approval requirements for proposed EDIRs and operators could be prescribed by the IRS in a revenue procedure. Thereafter, a uniform application could be designed and updated regularly by the IRS, subject to public comment and perhaps with the assistance of a citizens' advisory group like the ACT. In addition, the IRS could prescribe continuing approval requirements for previously approved EDIRs or operators, such as mandatory submissions of evidence regarding the frequency with which operators require the submission of updated information by foreign grantees. By engaging directly in individual applications for EDIR approval, of course, the IRS would be required to incur greater expense and dedicate more staff resources than it would under the "template EDIR" revenue procedure approach contemplated in the current ACT proposal. Nevertheless, the IRS currently provides

---

443   *E.g.*, disparate features in the repositories that yield differing degrees of comprehensiveness and/or accuracy in the content required by Rev. Proc. 92-94, such as the description of a foreign grantee's charitable purposes, schedules of financial data, or assurances concerning the absence of impermissible private inurement of the grantee's net assets.

individualized review of other private foundation proposals, including advance approval of grant making procedures for the purpose of avoiding taxable expenditures under Code section 49445(d)(3).[444] Moreover, such increased burdens on the IRS could be mitigated by one or more administrative techniques.

First, the IRS could establish application fees for EDIR applicants at a high enough level that would discourage frivolous applications, thereby reserving the IRS's scarce resources for the review of applications submitted by serious, qualified applicants. Current application fees established in connection with other types of rulings suggest that an appropriate fee might lie in the range of $5,000 to $7,500.[445] Second, the IRS could allow for "deemed approval" of proposed EDIRs after a certain period of time has elapsed following the submission of an application and until disposition of the application. The Treasury Regulations expressly adopt this technique, which admittedly favors taxpayers but provides some practical workflow relief to the IRS, in connection with applications for advance approval of scholarship procedures under Code section 4945.[446]

Finally, as previously proposed in related contexts,[447] the IRS could partially or wholly outsource the review of EDIR applications, as well as the oversight of continuing compliance by approved EDIR operators, to officially designated private partners who remain subject to IRS oversight and removal (if directly appointed by the IRS) or de-recognition (if previously recognized by the IRS as an approved authorizer of EDIRs or operators). Such nongovernmental "authorizers" are currently utilized in other regulatory contexts, such as Indiana's recognition of four-year colleges and universities, including private institutions, as "sponsors" or authorizers, i.e., quasi-regulators, of public charter schools.[448]

Moreover, the IRS allows reliance by private foundations on information repositories maintained by private operators for the purpose of verifying the public charity classification of proposed domestic grantees.[449] While the notion of a private body

---

444   See Rev. Proc. 2013-4, 2013-1 I.R.B. 126, 137 (section 7.04(10)).

445   See Rev. Proc. 2013-8, 2013-1 I.R.B. 237, 243-45 (sections 6.06(2) and 6.08) (the fee for a general request for a private letter ruling currently is $10,000, while the fee to seek advance approval of a scholarship procedure using Form 8940 is $1,000).

446   See Treas. Reg. sec. 53.4945-4(d)(3) (a scholarship procedure application is deemed approved 45 days after its submission to the IRS, unless and until the applicant has received notice from the IRS that the procedure is unacceptable). In light of the importance and broader implications of EDIR approval, the "deemed approved" date arguably should be much later than that used for scholarship procedures, e.g., something on the order of six months or one year.

447   See, e.g., Nina J. Crimm, Through a Post-September 11 Looking Glass: Assessing the Roles of Federal Tax Laws and Tax Policies Applicable to Global Philanthropy by Private Foundations and Their Donors, 23 Va. Tax Rev. 1, 157 (2003) (contemplating a "formal, industry-based self-regulatory body aimed at private foundations in global philanthropy," which could "share information on foreign grantees and equivalency determinations with all domestic private foundations").

448   See Indiana Code sec. 20-24-1-9(5).

449   See Rev. Proc. 2011-33, 2011-25 I.R.B. 887, 889 (section 4).

with regulatory powers always poses significant questions regarding the limits on power for such a body, the degree of oversight of the body by an actual governmental agency, and the standards for designation of or appointment to the body, the concept bears further investigation, particularly in the current fiscal context in which the approval of expansions of direct IRS oversight responsibilities is politically difficult to imagine.[450]

The time has come for the equivalency determination process to be stream-lined, standardized, and centralized. In light of technological advances, the development and maintenance of accurate, reliable, and accessible EDIRs is achievable. In addition, a legally official imprimatur for one or more authorized EDIRs or EDIR operators would allow private foundations to rely on their equivalency determinations for purposes of avoiding adverse consequences under the rules governing qualifying distributions and taxable expenditures.

Finally, the attributes of centralization, accessibility, and official recognition that would be associated with such EDIRs would facilitate more direct giving by private foundations to foreign charities, even (and perhaps particularly) where a prospective foreign grantee is not as well known to the private foundation or its proposed activities represent pioneering efforts that would stretch the private foundation's existing notions of program focus. Such dynamics would represent just the type of learning-driven philanthropy that would further each of the policy goals described at length in Chapter Five.

II. Deductibility for Individual and Corporate Charitable Gifts to Certain Foreign Grantees

United States tax law currently disallows deductions for individual and corporate gifts to a foreign charitable organization unless the foreign recipient possesses a determi-nation by the IRS of its tax-exempt status under United States tax law (a very rare cir-cumstance).[451] This limitation can be traced back to an era in which the United States maintained a relatively isolated stance in global affairs, having declined to join the League of Nations, and during which the country's attention continued to focus on the myriad domestic economic woes of the Great Depression.[452]

Fully three quarters of a century later, the tax law continues to reflect a 1938 world, notwithstanding multiple intervening epochal shifts in the global political and economic landscapes. Real concerns persist regarding the verification of the charitable

---

450   In this regard, the private EDIR authorizer could be supported in part by private funding sources. *Cf.* Crimm, *Through a Post-September 11 Looking Glass, supra* note 447, at p. 157 and n. 485 (observing that a self-regulatory body may need to be fully funded by private dues-paying private foundations).

451   *See* Code section 170(c)(2)(A) and discussion in section I of Chapter Three.

452   *See* the 1938 legislative history discussed in section I(1) of Chapter Three (H.R. Rep. No. 1860, 75th Cong., 3d Sess. 19-20 (1938)).

nature of prospective foreign grantees and their activities, as well as the potentially negative impact on domestic charitable endeavors created by increased international giving. Those concerns, however, can be adequately addressed through well-designed verification requirements and other limitations on the deductibility of individual and corporate charitable gifts made to non-United States charitable organizations.

As for the core policy rationale underlying the current wholesale prohibition on deductibility, however,[453] that rationale represents an antiquated relic of history. The prohibition not only predates our current notion of globalization; it constitutes a pre-Pearl Harbor artifact. It is time to bring this aspect of federal tax law into the twenty-first century.

Legal scholars have noted that while some Americans – both individuals and corporations – may make charitable gifts to foreign entities even in the absence of a corresponding federal income tax deduction, "global philanthropy is likely stimulated by the charitable contribution deduction."[454] Increased global philanthropy by Americans, particularly if undertaken in a learning-driven posture, could achieve several beneficial objectives.[455]

Specifically, increased levels of direct global philanthropic engagement could promote the national interests of the United States while also enhancing outcomes for individual donors and recipients such as increased effectiveness of charitable efforts in foreign countries, more innovation and risk taking in such charitable endeavors, and greater identification of donors with the recipients of their philanthropic support. The frequency and quality of such outcomes thus could be enhanced by encouraging greater levels of direct giving to foreign charities by Americans, which in turn could be stimulated by removing the existing general prohibition on the deductibility of such gifts from the taxable income of individuals and corporations.

Eliminating or mitigating the current total preclusion on deductibility for foreign charitable gifts made by individuals and corporations also could remove a counter-intuitive and illogical disparity in federal tax law. Private foundations currently may make grants to foreign organizations who meet the standards defining public charities under American tax law – subject, of course, to prior equivalency determinations or subsequent expenditure responsibility – using funds donated that they received from individuals and corporations, who in turn could deduct such original donations as charitable contributions.[456] Those individuals and corporations, however,

---

453   *See id.* ("The United States derives no ... benefit [*i.e.*, relief of financial burdens or the promotion of general welfare] from gifts to foreign institutions").

454   Crimm, *Through a Post-September 11 Looking Glass, supra* note 447, at pp. 137-38 and n. 80 (citing "[e]conometric studies demonstrat[ing] that, to some extent, charitable giving is price-elastic as well as connected to income level, and thus appears responsive to changes in tax rates").

455   *See generally* discussion in Chapter Five.

456   *See generally* discussion in section II of Chapter Three.

may not deduct gifts made directly to organizations that meet the definitional criteria of public charities under American tax law. In this regard, therefore, individuals and corporations are restricted from doing what private foundations can do.[457]

No overwhelming rationale supports this preferential treatment of private foundations relative to individuals and corporations. Waldemar Nielsen once reflected that "there is no more strange or improbable creature" in "the great jungle of American democracy and capitalism" than private foundations,[458] which generally are subject to stepped-up scrutiny and regulation rather than the favored status they enjoy in this instance. But these "strange [and] improbable creature[s]" offer the only practical means for individuals and corporations to engage in direct and deductible international philanthropy.

Of course, not nearly all individuals and businesses possess sufficient financial means and other resources to create or collaborate with private foundations. Most Americans, possessing more modest means and connections, do not enjoy such opportunities; indeed, many of them likely lack practical awareness of the role and legal features of private foundations, let alone the resources to create one. Such citizens, therefore, are limited in their international philanthropic efforts to working with American public charity intermediaries – and such intermediary arrangements typically result in reductions in the amounts ultimately transmitted to foreign recipients (because intermediaries must cover their costs) and require donors to cede control over the destination of their charitable contributions (as required by federal tax law).[459] By permitting limited deductibility for direct charitable gifts to foreign entities, this inequitable state of affairs could be remedied.

1.   Come Together: the Importance of Markets in Global Philanthropy and the Limits of Current Marketplace Efforts

Aside from tax law considerations, one traditional impediment to international philanthropic engagement has been the distributed nature of charitable activity in approximately two hundred countries worldwide, with little in the way of developed, centralized "marketplaces" through which information about such activity may be shared, evaluated, and supported. As described in 2007 by former World Bank executive Dennis Whittle,

---

457   Public charities, of course, also may make direct grants to foreign charities, and without the equivalency determinations or expenditure responsibility requirements that private foundations would need to observe. But for those seeking greater control over their philanthropic gifts, private foundations remain the only practical option. *See* Jerry J. McCoy and Kathryn W. Miree, *Family Foundation Handbook* (CCH, 2006), at sec. 2.02(A) ("there is one distinct tax advantage to be obtained through the creation of a foundation, and that is the manner in which a foundation enables a donor to achieve income tax deductions for expenditures that would not be deductible if made by an individual," including "grants to … foreign charities").

458   Waldemar A. Nielsen, *The Big Foundations* (Columbia University Press, 1972), p. 3.

459   *See* the discussion in the following section for a further discussion of these limitations.

Almost $2 trillion has been spent on foreign aid over the past 50 years. While some progress has been made in improving living standards (especially in a few larger countries such as China and India), there is a general consensus that the money has had far less impact than hoped. One reason for this has been the lack of a market mechanism, for allocating resources to the projects with the highest impact. Instead, the aid system has been divided up among a small number of organizations, which allocate resources based on a top-down approach that bears some similarities to central planning in the former Soviet Union.[460]

In this view, the absence of a developed market in global philanthropy seems to function as a catalyst for the traditional "Planner" mentality of foreign aid officials described by William Easterly,[461] and it also could partly account for the similarly prescriptive approach taken by many private philanthropists. By developing centralized instruments for gathering, sharing, and analyzing information on global charitable activity, such market barriers could be reduced or eliminated, while simultaneously promoting innovative charitable solutions from which established grant makers too often flinch – again, perhaps understandably so in light of the absence of efficient, accessible, and reliable mechanisms for evaluating the likely effectiveness of such proposed solutions.[462]

Online instruments such as GlobalGiving, co-founded by Dennis Whittle,[463] have begun to change the landscape for direct international philanthropy, allowing potential donors to screen prospective foreign grantees in a centralized database and then make a charitable gift for the benefit of one or more selected grantees. While such online repositories approximate direct giving, however, they do not offer a totally direct approach, because they are operated by United States charitable organizations that function as intermediaries so that donors may receive tax-deductible treatment for their gifts. As a consequence, less than all of the charitable donation makes its way to the foreign recipient. GlobalGiving, for instance, retains a 15 percent "fulfillment fee" to cover its costs of developing and maintaining the repository.[464] Moreover, tax

460   Dennis Whittle, "Markets for International Development," in Susan U. Raymond and Mary Beth Martin, eds., *Mapping the New World of American Philanthropy: Causes and Consequences of the Transfer of Wealth* (John Wiley & Sons, 2007), 167, 176-77.

461   *See generally* William Easterly, *The White Man's Burden: Why the West's Efforts to Aid the Rest Have Done So Much Ill and So Little Good* (The Penguin Press, 2006).

462   On the importance of innovation and entrepreneurial approaches to international charitable problem-solving, Whittle observes that "[o]ne of the most useful analogies is to think about how successful start-ups get launched, and then grow, in the United States. There is an ecosystem of investors who specialize in different stages of growth [but] [s]uch an ecosystem is only just now beginning to emerge in the international aid space." *Id.* at 177-78.

463   *See* "About GlobalGiving," http://www.globalgiving.org/aboutus/ (web site last visited on March 3, 2013).

464   "How GlobalGiving Works," http://www.globalgiving.org/howitworks.html (web sited last visited on March 3, 2013).

deductibility for donors to such intermediary organizations requires that the intermediary retain discretion over the use of the donor's gift.[465] Accordingly, the gift may in fact be used for purposes other than those contemplated by the donor, notwithstanding any promises to the contrary.[466]

2.   Widening the Circle of Deductibility Through the Use of Technology

If an American donor gives directly to a foreign grantee, rather than through an intermediary, two enhancements may be realized: the foreign organization receives more of the donated gift because the intermediary's costs are eliminated from the transaction, and the donor can be certain that the funds will not be diverted to another recipient by an intermediary exercising its legally required discretion. Of course, such direct gifts are discouraged by current federal tax law, which precludes the recognition of a charitable contribution deduction for gifts to a foreign organization under Code section 170(c)(2)(A) unless such organization has received a determination of tax-exempt status from the IRS.

By providing for deductibility in connection with such gifts in certain circumstances, federal tax law could offer an incentive to Americans – both individuals and corporations – to make contributions directly to foreign charities. Meanwhile, one of the most problematic features of international direct giving, the lack of a well-developed "marketplace," could be addressed through the very mechanism that also could facilitate effective legal regulation of deductible international philanthropy by individuals and corporations: official sanctioning of one or more EDIRs, which then could not only be used by private foundations for equivalency determinations but also could serve as a list of officially recognized grantees to whom individuals and corporations could make tax-deductible gifts, subject to appropriate limits.

Thus, the EDIR could be used to implement three significant objectives. First, the repository would provide private foundations and grantees with a centralized and effectively monitored[467] repository to facilitate international grant making by foundations. Second, an EDIR containing the information required for private foundation equivalency determinations – and updated on a regular basis by foreign grantees[468] as

---

465   See, e.g., Rev. Rul. 63-252, 1963-2 C.B. 101.

466   In practice, such diversions to other recipients rarely occur, for the very practical reason that they would tend to stem the flow of future funds from donors. Reputable providers such as GlobalGiving offer donors a choice of causes, rather than a choice of specific organizations, which largely eliminates this tax law problem. See, e.g., "How GlobalGiving Works," supra note 464.

467   Such monitoring could be implemented in conjunction with an application process prescribed by the IRS, and the monitoring function could be undertaken either by the IRS itself or through a self-regulation mechanism subject to IRS oversight. See recommendations discussed in section I(3) of this chapter.

468   Such repositories also could contain good faith determinations made by an expanded circle of qualified tax practitioners if the IRS adopts regulations that are still in proposed form at the time of this writing. See United States Department of the Treasury, Reliance Standards for Making Good Faith Deter-

required pursuant to Rev. Proc. 92-94 – would offer a fairly comprehensive and current database of information for individual and corporate donors seeking information about particular foreign organizations in connection with potential charitable gifts in the international arena.[469] And finally, an EDIR that qualifies for official recognition through a prescribed application process would offer a built-in regulatory tool for safeguarding the integrity of an expanded charitable contribution deduction available to individual and corporate donors wishing to engage in international philanthropy. This last function would reflect the utility of an EDIR to government, donors, and grantees alike as a mechanism for confirming on a continuing basis that the charitable organizations and activities funded by Americans in other countries meet applicable standards under applicable American tax laws.

3.   Addressing Challenges Associated with Expanded International Deductibility
        for Individuals and Corporations

Notwithstanding the obsolescence of the original rationale stated by legislators in support of the deduction exclusion now set forth in Code section 170(c)(2)(A), rooted as it was in the isolationism that colored much of American diplomacy and trade policy,[470] additional objections have been or could be raised to a general expansion of the charitable deduction to encompass direct charitable gifts by individuals and corporations to foreign grantees. Such objections include the complexity involved in verifying the charitable nature of foreign grantees and their activities, the prospect that federal deficits could be worsened if the tax base is shrunken through expanded deductions, and the potentially negative impact on domestic charities that could be caused by encouraging increased levels of international charitable giving by individuals and corporations. These objections are legitimate, and they must be addressed in any analysis of the prospective expansion of deductibility as proposed herein.

a.   The complexity objection

At least one prominent scholar of law and international philanthropy has articulated the first objection, *i.e.,* that allowing charitable contribution deductions in connection with direct charitable gifts made by individuals or corporations would be unworkable

---

minations, 77 Fed. Reg. 185 (proposed Sep. 24, 2012) (to be codified at 26 C.F.R. pt. 53); *see also* Notice of Proposed Rulemaking, Reliance Standards for Making Good Faith Determinations, REG–134974–12, 2012-47 I.R.B. 553 (Nov. 19, 2012).

469   In other words, an EDIR, while primarily conceived as a compliance tool, also could offer an entry point of information for curious individuals and corporations that could prompt further inquiries ultimately encouraging prospective donors to give to organizations about which they may not have known in the absence of the EDIR.

470   *See* H.R. Rep. No. 1860, 75th Cong., 3d Sess. 19-20 (1938). The view stated therein, that "[t]he United States derives no… benefit from gifts to foreign institutions," also reflects the relative paucity of international interconnectivity in the 1930s – in economic affairs, technology, communications, culture, and other areas - when compared to the pervasive levels of globalization that characterize today's world.

in light of the complexity inherent in making determinations as to the eligibility of proposed recipients or the suitability of the activities to be supported.[471] Such determinations are indeed complex, as evidenced by the IRS's perceived need to issue the "simplified" procedure for private foundations set forth in Rev. Proc. 92-94 and by calls for the recognition of EDIRs for the benefit of such foundations and their foreign grantees. But just as an increasingly interconnected world prompts more international philanthropic impulses on the part of all sorts of philanthropists – not just private foundations and public charities, but also individuals and corporations – the same interconnectivity facilitates increased levels of effectiveness, accuracy, and contemporaneity in ensuring the consistency of such activity with applicable federal tax law.

In addition, and as acknowledged by the same scholar, the marginal costs associated with private foundations' equivalency determinations decrease with subsequent additional determinations.[472] This phenomenon has prompted the call for EDIRs in the foundation world. For the same reason, individuals and corporations seeking to engage regularly in international philanthropy could utilize accurate, updated, and reasonably broad EDIRs. Furthermore, government regulators – by recognizing only EDIRs that meet significant requirements, which in turn could be established in a universal application published according to guidelines set forth in a revenue procedure – could have the same level of confidence in the integrity of individual and corporate gifts to foreign organizations listed in such EDIRs (and the consistency of such gifts with all applicable laws) as they have in grants made by private foundations using such EDIRs.[473]

In short, well-designed EDIRs, subject to tightly defined application and oversight processes for their official recognition, could allow individuals and corporations to benefit from equivalency determinations made by private foundations with more personnel, sophistication, and other resources. Conversely, by limiting individuals' and

---

471   See Nina J. Crimm, *Through a Post-September 11 Looking Glass: Assessing the Roles of Federal Tax Laws and Tax Policies Applicable to Global Philanthropy by Private Foundations and Their Donors*, 23 VA. TAX REV. 1 (2003) at n. 432, in which Crimm opposes deductibility for such gifts because "[d]iscerning whether the foreign organization actually is charitable or is utilizing the contributed funds for appropriate charitable purposes is difficult even for sophisticated public charities and domestic private foundations. These tasks likely would be even more difficult for individuals and corporations without connections, personnel, or experience abroad."

472   See *id.* at p. 127 ("[t]he burdens and costs associated with an initial grant and equivalency determination are high, but the burdens and costs associated with updating grantee information for purposes of subsequent grants are significantly less. Thus, [many] private foundations find an equivalency determination too costly and time consuming for one-shot grant relationships.").

473   As to any potential objection that it would be inappropriate to allow individuals and corporations to rely on determinations made by third parties and then contributed to an EDIR, such allowance already is extended to private foundations, who may rely on equivalency determinations based on affidavits provided to other private foundations. *See* Rev. Proc. 92-94, sec. 4.01. Moreover, the IRS has proposed that a private foundation may rely on a good faith determination made by any qualified tax practitioner, not just the foundation's own legal counsel. *See* United States Department of the Treasury, Reliance Standards for Making Good Faith Determinations, and Notice of Proposed Rulemaking, REG–134974–12, *supra* note 468.

corporations' deductibility to direct charitable gifts made to foreign organizations listed in officially recognized EDIRs, government and the general public could maintain a high level of confidence that the complexities of equivalency determinations would not compromise the integrity of such deductions.[474]

By limiting deductibility in this manner, the encouragement of greater levels of international philanthropic activity by individuals and corporations likewise would be limited. In the future, however, with the development of additional and even more accessible tools for collecting, sharing, and evaluating information about global charitable activity, perhaps the limits of individual and corporate deductibility could be further expanded to encompass gifts made using such additional tools, even where they are not designed primarily with private foundations in mind.[475]

b.   The federal deficit exacerbation objection

In the current fiscal environment, legislators and taxpayers alike may be reluctant to reduce the tax base further by expanding the limits of charitable contribution deductions as proposed herein. Although it is beyond the scope of this book to project the likely effect on the federal treasury of allowing general deductibility for charitable gifts made by individuals and corporations to foreign charities, it is reasonable to assume some level of net cost to the public fisc, even if such giving partially replaces some government-sponsored foreign aid programs.

Budget-driven concerns could be mitigated by placing limits on the extent of such deductibility. Such limits could be reflected in absolute dollar value ceilings, pursuant to which no more than a prescribed amount (e.g., $10,000) of such gifts would be eligible for deductibility in any tax year. Alternatively, the limits could be percentage-based, e.g., no more than 25 percent of all charitable deductions recognized by an individual or a corporation may correspond to gifts made to foreign charities. One particularly interesting alternative might feature an incentive for repetitive involvement in international charitable giving, thereby deterring individuals and corporations from "one-off" gifts that may exacerbate sustainability challenges for foreign charities. Such an incentive, which could double as a budget relief tool by quantitatively limiting deductions associated with international giving, might require an individual or a corporation to verify previous direct and non-deductible charitable gifts to foreign organizations identified in a recognized EDIR in one or more previous

---

474   Educational outreach efforts, which could be undertaken by philanthropy interest groups such as the Council on Foundations and by academic institutions, could augment the public's understanding of such new deductibility rules and could help explain the role of EDIRs in broadly accessible terms.

475   In this manner, individuals and corporations would not be relegated to "piggybacking" on information first developed by, or primarily for the benefit of, private foundations.

tax years, or a certain minimum amount of such charitable gifts made in previous tax years, before deductibility would be allowed for subsequent gifts.[476]

An even more experimental approach could require some sort of evidence of active conduct or service on behalf of the foreign charity by the taxpayer requesting the deduction in order to claim a deduction for charitable gifts to the charity.[477] Such a mandate could be fulfilled with personal service to the charity in the foreign country, or it could be met through some sort of advocacy-related activity in the United States, e.g., presenting information about the charity's efforts in public forums or participating in fundraising events designed to raise support from the general public. The chief challenges associated with this approach would include the inherent difficulties and potential inequities in categorizing permissible activities or service and verifying the time spent for purposes of meeting a required threshold associated with the deductibility of gifts. Perhaps even more significantly in a policy sense, this requirement could produce discriminatory effects toward those whose work requirements, family commitments, or physical limitations make it more difficult to render active service on behalf of the charity. On the other hand, such a requirement would seem to promote the salutary effect of more charitable activity in tandem with charitable giving.[478]

c.   The "charity begins at home" objection

Encouraging more and better international philanthropy by individuals and corporations – particularly philanthropy of the learning-driven variety – could produce a number of desirable effects for foreign recipients, the United States' national interests, and donors themselves.[479] Nevertheless, limitless philanthropic resources do not exist in the United States or anywhere else, and to the extent Americans respond to tax incentives by increasing their international charitable giving, it is possible that domestic charities could experience a corresponding downturn in support.

---

476   Such an approach essentially would reflect the inverse of the first proposed alternative by disallowing the first tranche of foreign charitable contributions rather than any such contributions beyond a specified threshold. Either approach, however, would tend to limit the extent of federal tax revenue lost through the expansion of the charitable contribution deduction.

477   This notion borrows from the requirements associated with qualification as a private operating foundation under Code section 4942(j)(3). Operating foundations are required to expend a certain amount of funds each year (measured under alternative mathematical tests) on "qualifying distributions ... directly for the active conduct of the activities constituting [its charitable] purpose or function." Code section 4942(j)(3)(A) (emphasis added). Generally, the making of grants to support the conduct of charitable activities by other entities will not satisfy the "active conduct" requirement applicable to operating foundations. See Treas. Reg. sec. 53.4942(b)-1(b)(1).

478   As noted earlier, Robert Putnam has noted that in building healthy social capital, "volunteering and philanthropy are complements, not substitutes." Robert D. Putnam, Bowling Alone: The Collapse and Revival of American Community (Simon & Schuster, 2000), at p. 118.

479   See Chapter Five for further discussion.

Several possible legal devices could help limit the potential harm to domestic charities.[480] First, the charitable contribution deduction allowance for direct international gifts could be conditioned on a "matching" domestic giving requirement or some other minimum level of domestic charitable giving, which could represent a fraction or a multiple of the requested deduction for international gifts. Under this approach, individuals or corporations would be required to demonstrate some specified amount of domestic charitable giving relative to their requested deduction for international giving (whether one-for-one, or some other ratio).[481]

A second possible limitation would involve a variation on the notion of an "active conduct" requirement for individuals, in this case conditioning deductibility for charitable gifts to foreign entities on active service in support of one or more qualified *domestic* charities. Such a requirement also could be implemented in tandem with the matching gift requirement described above, with some substitutability of service to domestic charities in lieu of charitable gifts. As noted in the earlier discussion of an active conduct requirement, however, serious problems would seem to exist in the verification, quantification, and categorization of permissible service activities, in addition to the potential policy objection that often the most effective volunteer workers may not be the same individuals who have the financial capacity to make charitable contributions. For these reasons, any effort to protect domestic charities from excessive damage as a result of increased international giving seems better based on a matching or percentage-based domestic giving requirement, rather than a service-based approach to conditional deductibility.

4.   The Legal Mechanics of Expanding Deductibility to the International Arena

From a process standpoint, the expansion of deductibility to encompass certain charitable gifts made directly to foreign charities by individuals or corporations theoretically could be achieved through one of several different legal mechanisms. First, the United States could enter into additional bilateral or multilateral tax treaties similar to the treaties currently in place with Mexico, Canada, and Israel.[482] Such a piecemeal approach, however, would not offer uniformity or predictability. Nor would it be designed to promote effectively the increased international philanthropic engagement advocated herein, as the provisions of treaties typically are not part of the common knowledge of the average American – or even the knowledge of many Americans with

---

480   These devices could be implemented in addition to the limits or prerequisites described in the immediately preceding section.

481   In effect, a one-for-one "matching" requirement would operate as a 50 percent limitation on the portion of charitable contribution deductions that could be recognized in connection with international gifts.

482   The existing treaties, however, largely limit deductibility to the extent of income generated in the respective foreign countries. See discussion *supra* in section I(1) of Chapter Three. The approach recommended herein would require more expansive treaties that do not contain such foreign-source income-based limitations.

high levels of sophistication in tax planning. Finally, such an approach historically has met with legislative resistance, making its adoption unlikely.[483]

A more plausible approach would involve amending Code section 170(c)(2)(A), which currently describes gifts made to certain organizations "created or organized in the United States or in any possession thereof, or under the law of the United States, any State, the District of Columbia, or any possession of the United States." To this text could be added a disjunctive phrase that describes – and circumscribes – a group of foreign organizations. Accordingly, subparagraph (A) could be subdivided into parts (i) and (ii). Part (i) would contain the same text described above, which currently appears in (A) ("created or organized in the United States …"), followed by the word "or," and part (ii) could include words to the following effect: "created or organized in or under the laws of another country, subject to [limitations described in a cross-referenced separate section of the Internal Revenue Code and/or regulations promulgated by the Secretary of the Treasury]." In turn, the limitations prescribed elsewhere in statutory language and/or in Treasury Regulations could address the challenges of complexity and verification for individuals and corporations lacking the resources of private foundations, the prospective depletion of the tax base, and the potential siphoning of funds from domestic charities.[484]

In summary, the time has come to end the geographic bifurcation that currently characterizes the laws governing the deductibility of charitable gifts by individuals and

---

483   See Nina J. Crimm, Through a Post-September 11 Looking Glass: Assessing the Roles of Federal Tax Laws and Tax Policies Applicable to Global Philanthropy by Private Foundations and Their Donors, 23 VA. TAX REV. 1, 47 and n. 138 (2003) ("[t]he Senate Committee on Foreign Relations … has repeatedly expressed reservations on the wholesale inclusion of a bilateral income tax treaty provision that would permit a United States citizen … or domestic corporation to claim an income tax charitable contribution deduction when making donations directly to a foreign charitable organization" (citing legislative history in connection with treaty negotiations with Brazil and Canada)).

484   Unfortunately, some of the language used by the IRS to explain recently proposed amendments to the "good faith determination" regulations suggests that the use of affidavits by foreign grantees could be in jeopardy altogether. See United States Department of the Treasury, Reliance Standards for Making Good Faith Determinations, 77 Fed. Reg. 185 (proposed Sep. 24, 2012) (to be codified at 26 C.F.R. pt. 53) ("[b]ecause the [proposed allowance of good faith determination opinions by any qualified tax practitioner, rather than only by the foundation's own legal counsel] is expected to make it easier and less costly to … make a good faith determination, the Treasury Department and the IRS also are considering whether it is appropriate to further amend the current regulations to remove the ability of a private foundation to base a good faith determination on an affidavit of a foreign grantee"). The IRS has expressed concern on this point, however, noting that "eliminating the ability to base a good faith determination on an affidavit of a foreign grantee may inappropriately discourage foreign grantmaking by smaller private foundations, or inhibit smaller foreign grants generally." Id. Consistent with the objectives and rationales articulated throughout this paper, a preferable approach would allow the use of both types of good faith determinations, i.e., by qualified tax practitioners and by foreign grantees, and compiling such determinations in regularly updated and certified EDIRs as described above.

corporations.[485] The rationales undergirding the non-deductibility of such gifts to foreign charitable entities are outdated and incongruent with the United States' role in contemporary global affairs. The challenges presented by an expanded deduction could be satisfactorily met via technology (*e.g.*, well-designed and properly maintained EDIRs) and by limitations built into the applicable statutory or regulatory provisions in order to address concerns regarding fiscal impact and adverse effects on domestic charities. Finally, the allowance of deductions in this context will promote more direct global philanthropic engagement by individuals and corporations, which in turn can be undertaken in a learning-driven posture that empowers and dignifies the foreign beneficiaries of such philanthropy while achieving the goals of effectiveness, innovation, identification, promotion of American national interests, and relief of government and international organizations.

---

485   Although not analyzed herein, this call for change also could encompass an end to the geographic use limitation that currently renders non-deductible any corporate charitable gifts to domestic unincorporated entities that are subsequently used to support activities outside the United States. *See* Code section 170(c)(2) ("flush-left" language).

Conclusion

The legal framework governing American philanthropy reflects a robust, well-developed system commensurate with the broad and diverse patterns of giving established throughout American history. On the domestic front, the American philanthropic sector is both stimulated and effectively governed by a sprawling structure of interlocking legal schemes at the federal, state, and local levels. Through tax exemptions awarded to charitable organizations, donors' ability to deduct most charitable gifts from their federal taxable income, and other avenues, the law effectively encourages domestic generosity by Americans to fellow Americans. Conversely, American laws efficaciously regulate all aspects of charitable activity – including (but not limited to) the solicitation of charitable contributions, the allowance of income tax deductions for donors making such contributions, and the use of such tax-free dollars by the organizations that enjoy exemption from entity-level income taxation. Domestically speaking, the balance between encouragement and regulation has been struck about as finely and effectively as one could imagine in light of the complexity and multiplicity of laws and legal systems that affect philanthropy.

Beyond American borders, however, the balance of laws governing philanthropic activity tips heavily toward enforcement and away from encouragement. Private foundations may make grants to foreign grantees, but only if they undertake the exhaustive, costly, and time-consuming process of equivalency determination (or, alternatively, the equally onerous process of expenditure responsibility) – and currently, no effective centralized repository exists for equivalency determinations, with the result that private foundations typically must undertake fresh equivalency determinations for each contemplated grant to a foreign entity (or rely on another private foundation's equivalency determination for the same entity). Public charities may support foreign charitable activity with fewer restrictions on the payment of grants, but in raising funds for such efforts, they generally may not promise to earmark or otherwise designate funds solicited from individuals, corporations, and others for specific international programs.

Individuals and corporations, in turn, arguably labor under the tightest restrictions of all in the international philanthropic context, as they generally may not recognize federal income tax deductions in connection with charitable gifts to foreign charities. Accordingly, for all practical purposes, individuals and corporations seeking to support international charitable endeavors are limited to making gifts to American intermediary public charities, which in turn are required by law to exercise control over those gifts to ensure consistency with the American charities' purposes (which may not necessarily be identical to the supported foreign charities' purposes). Moreover, the requisite use of intermediaries by American citizens and corporations seeking deductibility for their internationally-intended charitable gifts means that fewer dollars reach the ultimate foreign destination, as the intermediaries must cover their administrative costs associated with soliciting, managing, and redistributing such gifts.

I maintain that Americans should be encouraged to modify their patterns of international philanthropy to reflect a more "learning-driven" posture of charitable giving in which the wisdom of foreign grantees is given primacy with respect to the selection of charitable objectives and the operational methodologies utilized to achieve those objectives. Such an approach requires the reconsideration of international philanthropic engagement by American public charities and private foundations, which currently tend to select international projects based on their propensity to help realize objectives established by American grant makers rather than foreign beneficiaries.

A more learning-driven approach to international philanthropy would further several important policy objectives, including the stimulation of more effective and innovative charitable efforts to meet the most difficult challenges faced in foreign countries (particularly those in the developing world); the encouragement of closer identification between donors and beneficiaries, which itself represents one of the most significant motivations for any philanthropic activity; the promotion of the national interests of the United States through the projection of benign "soft power"; and the relief of burdens on the overstretched budgets of federal government agencies responsible for foreign aid as well as many international organizations who depend heavily on the United States government for support.

American grant makers currently tend to base their international philanthropic engagement on their own independently defined objectives and operational presumptions. These patterns closely align with the current American legal framework. As noted above, that framework essentially requires international grants to further the purposes of the grant maker, particularly in the context of intermediary public charities' utilization of funds raised from individual and corporate donors. Accordingly, by altering the American legal framework applicable to international philanthropy in a few key but discrete respects, law and policy can be pursued harmoniously to bring antiquated American laws into alignment with twenty-first century global realities while promoting more direct and learning-driven charitable giving by American private foundations, public charities, individuals, and corporations.

Two main legal reforms could help achieve these objectives. First, a mechanism should be described in a broadly applicable revenue procedure or similar means and then published in a universal application format that serves as a tool for providing official recognition of electronic equivalency determination information repositories ("EDIRs"). Private foundations could use such EDIRs as a more efficient, less costly, and more accurate means of ensuring that grants to foreign charities constitute qualifying distributions and avoiding confiscatory excise taxes under the taxable expenditure rules. In this manner, the creation of an EDIR recognition procedure could stimulate more and better international grant making by private foundations.

Second, the general prohibition on income tax deductions in connection with charitable gifts made by individuals and corporations directly to foreign charities should be significantly alleviated. Deductibility under such circumstances could be predicated on the foreign charities' inclusion in an EDIR officially recognized via the process contemplated above. This approach would effectively address concerns related to the complexity of the equivalency determination process and the accompanying fear that deductions otherwise could be inappropriately recognized by individual and corporate donors in connection with gifts to non-qualified foreign recipients. With respect to concerns regarding the negative impact of such expanded deductibility on federal tax revenues or financial support to domestic charities, several limitation mechanisms could be adopted, including percentage-based limits, domestic matching requirements, and/or service-based prerequisites.

Although it may require time to refine such reforms and limitations more precisely, that challenge should not deter all efforts to pursue sorely needed reforms to the American laws governing international philanthropy. It is time to prompt more effective "yearning and striving"[486] by Americans on the global stage. These reforms can help propel us in that direction.

---

486   Steve Corbett and Brian Fikkert, *When Helping Hurts: Alleviating Poverty Without Hurting the Poor ... and Yourself* (Moody Publishers, 2009), at p. 29.

Bibliography

"About GlobalGiving," http://www.globalgiving.org/aboutus/ (web site last visited on March 3, 2013)

Advisory Committee on Tax Exempt and Government Entities, "Exempt Organizations: Recommendations to Improve the Tax Rules Governing International Grantmaking" (June 10, 2009), http://www.irs.gov/pub/irs-tege/tege_act_rpt8.pdf

Advisory Committee on Tax Exempt and Government Entities, "Exempt Organizations: Form 1023 – Updating It for the Future" (June 6, 2012), http://www.irs.gov/pub/irs-tege/tege_act_rpt11.pdf

Alliance for Charitable Reform, "An Active Week in Washington on the Charitable Deduction" (Anne Urban, "Consider This …" Blog), Feb. 22, 2013, http://acreform.com/blog/an_active_week_in_washington_on_the_charitable_deduction/ (web site last visited on March 3, 2013)

Alliance for Charitable Reform, "U.K. Abandons Plan to Curb Tax Incentives," June 1, 2012, http://acreform.com/blog/u.k._considers_plan_to_limit_charitable_giving_incentive/ (web site last visited on March 3, 2013)

A Taxonomic Tree of Philanthropy, CATALOGUE FOR PHILANTHROPY, http://www.catalogueforphilanthropy.org/ma/2007/05_taxonomic_tree_of_philanthropy.html

Barry, Ellen, *As 'Foreign Agent' Law Takes Effect in Russia, Human Rights Groups Vow to Defy It*, NEW YORK TIMES (Nov. 21, 2012) (http://www.nytimes.com/2012/11/22/world/europe/rights-groups-in-russia-reject-foreign-agent-label.html?_r=0)

Barry, Ellen, *Foreign-Funded Nonprofits in Russia Face New Hurdle*, NEW YORK TIMES (July 2, 2012) (http://www.nytimes.com/2012/07/03/world/europe/russia-introduces-law-limiting-aid-for-nonprofits.html)

Barry, Ellen, *Russian Legislators Approve Greater Government Control Over the Internet and Nonprofits*, NEW YORK TIMES (July 18, 2012) (http://www.nytimes.com/2012/07/19/world/europe/russian-parliament-approves-greater-government-control-over-the-internet-and-nonprofits.html)

Bellah, Robert N., et al., *Habits of the Heart: Individualism and Commitment in American Life* (Harper & Row, 1985)

Besley, Timothy, Review Essay, *Poor Choices: Poverty from the Ground Level*, 91 FOREIGN AFFAIRS 160 (2012)

Bjorklund, Victoria B., and Joanna Pressman, "Cross-Border Philanthropy," in Penina Kessler Lieber and Donald R. Levy, eds., *Complete Guide to Nonprofit Organizations* (Civic Research Institute, 2005)

Blanton, Ben W., "Introduction to Tax-Exempt Organizations," *Exempt Organizations and Charitable Activities in Indiana* (National Business Institute, 1992)

Bolton, Giles, *Africa Doesn't Matter: How the West Has Failed the Poorest Continent and What We Can Do About It* (Arcade, 2007)

Bono, *The Resource Miracle*, TIME (May 28, 2012) (http://www.time.com/time/magazine/article/0,9171,2115044,00.html)

Boulding, Kenneth, *The Economy of Love and Fear: A Preface to Grants Economics* (Wadsworth, 1973)

Boulding, Kenneth, *Three Faces of Power* (Sage Publications, 1989)

Broadway Theatre League of Lynchburg, Va., Inc. v. United States, 293 F. Supp. 346 (W.D. Va. 1968)

Callison, J. William, & Allan W. Vestal, *The L3C Illusion: Why Low-Profit Limited Liability Companies Will Not Stimulate Socially Optimal Private Foundation Investment in Entrepreneurial Ventures*, 35 VERMONT L. REV. 273 (2010)

Center on Philanthropy at Indiana University, *The 2010 Study of High Net Worth Philanthropy* (2010), available at http://www.philanthropy.iupui.edu/research-by-category/the-2010-study-of-high-net-worth-philanthropy

Cesare, Laura Watson, "Private Foundations and Public Charities – Definition and Classification," 876 Tax Mgmt. (BNA) Estates, Gifts, and Trusts, at A-1 (2000)

Charity Navigator, "How Do We Classify Charities?" http://www.charitynavigator.org/index.cfm?bay=content.view&cpid=34 (web site last visited on March 3, 2013)

Chiu, Lisa, *Nonprofits Oppose Obama Plan on Limiting Charity Write-Offs*, THE CHRONICLE OF PHILANTHROPY/PHILANTHROPY TODAY (Feb. 13, 2012), http://philanthropy.com/article/Nonprofits-Oppose-Obama-Plan/130776/

Clark, Gregory, "But Wait! Can't the Poor Decide for Themselves?," in Kinsley, Michael, and Conor Clarke, eds., *Creative Capitalism* (Simon & Schuster, 2008)

Collier, Paul, *The Bottom Billion: Why the Poorest Countries are Failing and What Can Be Done About It* (Oxford, 2007)

Commissioner v. Duberstein, 363 U.S. 278 (1960)

A Convention Between the United States of America and Canada with Respect to Taxes on Income and on Capital, effective as of January 1, 1985 (available at http://unclefed.com/ForTaxProfs/Treaties/index.html) (web site last visited on March 3, 2013)

The Convention Between the Government of the United States of America and the Government of the United Mexican States for the Avoidance of Double Taxation and the Prevention of Fiscal Evasion with Respect to Taxes on Income, Together with a Related Protocol, effective as of January 1, 1994 (available at http://unclefed.com/ForTaxProfs/Treaties/index.html) (web site last visited on March 3, 2013)

Convention Between the Government of the United States of America and the Government of the State of Israel with Respect to Taxes on Income, Protocol 1, Article X, executed on May 30 and June 2, 1980 (available at http://unclefed.com/ForTaxProfs/Treaties/index.html) (web site last visited on March 3, 2013)

Corbett, Steve, and Brian Fikkert, *When Helping Hurts: Alleviating Poverty Without Hurting the Poor … and Yourself* (Moody Publishers, 2009)

Crimm, Nina J., *Democratization, Global Grant-Making, and the Internal Revenue Code Lobbying Restrictions*, 79 TUL. L. REV. 587 (2005)

Crimm, Nina J., *Global Philanthropy Depends on Tax Laws*, THE CHRONICLE OF PHILANTHROPY (Apr. 3, 2003), http://philanthropy.com/article/Global-Philanthropy-Depends-on/49750/

Crimm, Nina J., *Through a Post-September 11 Looking Glass: Assessing the Roles of Federal Tax Laws and Tax Policies Applicable to Global Philanthropy by Private Foundations and Their Donors*, 23 VA. TAX REV. 1 (2003)

Curry, Tom, *Kerry: Foreign Aid is in America's self-interest*, NBCNews.com (February 20, 2013) (http://nbcpolitics.nbcnews.com/_news/2013/02/20/17031977-kerry-foreign-aid-is-in-americas-self-interest?lite)

De Tocqueville, Alexis, *Democracy in America* (Penguin Books translation, 2003)

Di Mento, Maria, *Big Companies Slowly Increase Their Charitable Giving*, THE CHRONICLE OF PHILANTHROPY/THE GIVEAWAY (June 5, 2012)

Downturn Forces Disease Fund to Suspend New Grants, THE CHRONICLE OF PHILANTHROPY/PHILANTHROPY TODAY (Nov. 28, 2011), http://philanthropy.com/blogs/philanthropy-today/downturn-forces-disease-fund-to-suspend-new-grants/42390

Durden v. Commissioner, T.C. Memo. 2012-140

Ealy, Steven D., Research Note, *Taxation as a One-Way Transfer? A Note on a Conceptual Confusion in Kenneth Boulding*, 4 CONVERSATIONS ON PHILANTHROPY 47 (Donors Trust, 2007)

Easterly, William, *The White Man's Burden: Why the West's Efforts to Aid the Rest Have Done So Much Ill and So Little Good* (The Penguin Press, 2006)

Egypt Denies Licenses for 8 U.S.-Based Nonprofits, THE CHRONICLE OF PHILANTHROPY/PHILANTHROPY TODAY (Apr. 24, 2012), http://philanthropy.com/blogs/philanthropytoday/egypt-denies-licenses-for-8-u-s-based-nonprofits/46777

Emmert, Frank, "Market Economy, Democracy, or Rule of Law? What Should Be Prioritized to Promote Development?", in Astrid Epiney, Marcel Haag and Andreas Heinemann eds., *Challenging Boundaries – Essays in Honor of Roland Bieber* (Nomos, 2007)

Esposito, John L. *Ten Things to Know About Islam* (Middle East Policy Council), http://www.teach-mideast.org/essays/35-religion/58-ten-things-to-know-about-islam

Etheridge, Jr., Donald McGee, "Private Foundations – Section 4940 and Section 4944," 468 Tax Mgmt. (BNA) Estates, Gifts, and Trusts, A-1 (2011)

Freda, Diane, *Pease Amendment on Itemized Deductions Alive and Well and Scheduled for 2013*, BLOOMBERG BNA DAILY TAX REPORT, May 29, 2012

Freda, Diane, *Private Foundations Ask IRS to Allow Repository for Foreign Grant Information*, BLOOMBERG BNA DAILY TAX REPORT, May 2, 2012

Freda, Diane, *Program-Related Investment Guidance Adds More Current Examples for Exempts*, BLOOMBERG BNA DAILY TAX REPORT, Apr. 20, 2012

Freitag, Carla Neeley, "Unrelated Business Income Tax," 462 Tax Mgmt. (BNA) Estates, Gifts, and Trusts, at A-1 (2009)

Fremont-Smith, Marion R., *Governing Nonprofit Organizations: Federal and State Law and Regulation* (The Belknap Press of Harvard University Press, 2004)

French, Howard W., *The Next Empire*, THE ATLANTIC (May 2010), available online at http://www.theatlantic.com/magazine/archive/2010/05/the-next-empire/308018/

Fund Halts New Grants for AIDS, TB and Malaria Treatment in Poor Countries, WASHINGTON POST (Nov. 23, 2011), http://www.washingtonpost.com/national/health-science/fund-halts-new-grants-for-aidstb-and-malaria-treatment-in-poor-countries/2011/11/23/glQAPZdspN_story.html

Gallagher, Janne G., *Grantmaking in an Age of Terrorism: Some Thoughts about Compliance Strategies*, 70 International Dateline (Council on Foundations, 2004) (available at http://www.cof.org/templates/content.cfm?itemnumber=12696&navItemNumber=15633)

Gose, Ben, *IRS Urged to Reduce Paperwork Burden on Charities*, THE CHRONICLE OF PHILANTHROPY/TAX WATCH (MAY 16, 2012), http://philanthropy.com/article/IRS-Urged-to-Reduce-Paperwork/131899/

Hamilton County Property Tax Assessment Board of Appeals v. Oaken Bucket Partners, LLC, 938 N.E.2d 654 (Ind. 2010)

Hansmann, Henry, *The Rationale for Exempting Nonprofit Organizations From Corporate Income Taxation*, 91 YALE L.J. 54 (1981)

Herszenhorn, David M., and Andrew Roth, *Russian Law Would Place Tougher Restrictions on Nonprofits*, NEW YORK TIMES (July 13, 2012) (http://www.nytimes.com/2012/07/14/world/europe/russian-law-would-place-tougher-restrictions-on-nonprofits.html?pagewanted=all)

Holy Bible (New Living Translation; Tyndale House Foundation, 2007)

Hopkins, Bruce R., "Law and Taxation," in Tracy Daniel Connors, ed., *The Nonprofit Handbook: Management*, 3d ed. (John Wiley & Sons, 2001)

Hopkins, Bruce R., *The Law of Tax-Exempt Organizations*, 10th ed. (John Wiley & Sons, 2011 & 2012 Supplement)

Hopkins, Bruce R., *The Law of Tax-Exempt Organizations Planning Guide: Strategies and Commentaries* (John Wiley & Sons, 2004)

Hopkins, Bruce R., *The Tax Law of Charitable Giving*, 4th ed. (John Wiley & Sons, 2010)

Hopkins, Bruce R., *The Tax Law of Unrelated Business for Nonprofit Organizations* (John Wiley & Sons, 2005)

Hopkins, Bruce R., and Jody Blazek, *The Legal Answer Book for Private Foundations* (John Wiley & Sons, 2002)

Hopkins, Bruce R. and Jody Blazek, *Private Foundations: Tax Law and Compliance*, 3d ed. (John Wiley & Sons, 2008)

"How GlobalGiving Works," http://www.globalgiving.org/howitworks.html (web site last visited on March 3, 2013)

Hoyt, Christopher R., *Legal Compendium for Community Foundations* (Council on Foundations, 1991)

H.R. 9682, 75th Cong., Pub. L. 75-554 (1938)

H.R. 13270, 91st Cong., Pub. L. 91-172 (1970)

H.R. Rep. No. 1860, 75th Cong., 3d Sess. 19-20 (1938) (emphasis added) (as quoted in *Hopkins, The Tax Law of Charitable Giving,* 4th ed. (John Wiley & Sons, 2010), at pp. 600-01

Indiana Code (various sections)

Internal Revenue Service, *Exempt Organizations Annual Reporting Requirements – Form 990, Schedule R: "Related Organization" and "Controlled Entity" Reporting Differences,* http://www.irs.gov/Charities-&-Non-Profits/Exempt-Organizations-Annual-Reporting-Requirements---Form-990,-Schedule-R:---Related-Organization--and--Controlled-Entity--Reporting-Differences (web site last visited on March 3, 2013)

Internal Revenue Service, *Exempt Organizations Annual Reporting Requirements – Form 990, Schedule R: Reporting Related Party Transactions,* http://www.irs.gov/Charities-&-Non-Profits/Exempt-Organizations-Annual-Reporting-Requirements---Form-990,-Schedule-R:-Reporting-Related-Party-Transactions (web site last visited on March 3, 2013)

Internal Revenue Service Form 990 and related schedules (2011)

Internal Revenue Service Form 990-PF and related schedules (2011)

Internal Revenue Service Form 1023, Application for Recognition of Exemption Under Section 501(c)(3) of the Internal Revenue Code (June 2006)

Internal Revenue Service, *IRS Identifies Organizations that Have Lost Tax-Exempt Status; Announces Special Steps to Help Revoked Organizations* (June 9, 2011) (http://www.irs.gov/uac/IRS-Identifies-Organizations-that-Have-Lost-Tax-Exempt-Status%3B-Announces-Special-Steps-to-Help-Revoked-Organizations) (web site last visited on March 3, 2013)

Internal Revenue Service Publication 526, *Charitable Contributions* (2011)

Internal Revenue Service, *Understanding IRS Guidance – A Brief Primer,* http://www.irs.gov/uac/Understanding-IRS-Guidance---A-Brief-Primer (web site last visited on March 3, 2013)

Internal Revenue Service General Counsel Memorandum 37444 (March 7, 1978)

The International Center for Not-for-Profit Law, *NGO Law Monitor: Russia,* http://www.icnl.org/research/monitor/russia.html (web site last visited on March 3, 2013)

IRS Rules Would Allow Private Foundations to Make Range of Charitable Investments, BLOOMBERG BNA DAILY TAX REPORT, Apr. 19, 2012

Jackson, William J., *Seven Myths of Philanthropy; Seven Opportunities in Understanding,* 7 CONVERSATIONS ON PHILANTHROPY 25 (Donors Trust, 2010)

Jewell, Katherine C., "When Charities Behave Badly: State Attorneys General on the Case," in Raymond, Susan U., and Mary Beth Martin, eds., *Mapping the New World of American Philanthropy: Causes and Consequences of the Transfer of Wealth* (John Wiley & Sons, 2007)

Kanani, Rahim, *Laura Arrillaga-Andreessen on 21st Century Philanthropy and Smarter Giving*, FORBES (May 24, 2012), http://www.forbes.com/sites/rahimkanani/2012/05/24/laura-arrillaga-andreessen-on-21st-century-philanthropy-and-smarter-giving/

Kirkpatrick, David D., *Egypt Rejects Registration Bids from 8 U.S. Nonprofit Groups*, NEW YORK TIMES (Apr. 23, 2012) (http://www.nytimes.com/2012/04/24/world/middleeast/egypt-rejects-registration-bids-from-8-us-nonprofits.html?_r=1)

Korenchuk, Keith M., James P. Joseph, Samuel M. Witten, and Andras Kosaras, *Guarding Against Anti-Corruption Problems in Overseas Philanthropic Activities*, TAXATION OF EXEMPTS, Nov./Dec. 2011, 19

Lieber, Penina Kessler, "The Nonprofit Organization – Its Form and Structure," in Penina Kessler Lieber and Donald R. Levy, eds., *Complete Guide to Nonprofit Organizations* (Civic Research Institute, 2005)

Lewis, Paul, *Commitment, Identity, and Collective Intentionality: The Basis for Philanthropy*, 6 CONVERSATIONS ON PHILANTHROPY 47 (Donors Trust, 2009)

Lloyd, Gordon, *Boulding's Global-Socialist Theory of Philanthropy*, 4 CONVERSATIONS ON PHILANTHROPY 1 (Donors Trust, 2007)

Madigan v. Telemarketing Associates, 538 U.S. 600 (2003)

McCray, Richard A., and Ward L. Thomas, *Limited Liability Companies as Exempt Organizations* – Update, 2001 Exempt Organizations Continuing Professional Education Text 27

McCully, George, *Philanthropy and Humanity*, 7 CONVERSATIONS ON PHILANTHROPY 43 (Donors Trust, 2010)

McCoy, Jerry J., and Kathryn W. Miree, *Family Foundation Handbook* (CCH, 2006)

Moyo, Dambisa, *Dead Aid: Why Aid is Not Working and How There Is a Better Way Forward for Africa* (Farrar, Straus and Giroux, 2009)

Nielsen, Waldemar, *The Big Foundations* (Columbia University Press, 1972)

Nielsen, Waldemar, *The Golden Donors* (E.P. Dutton, 1985)

Notice of Proposed Rulemaking, Reliance Standards for Making Good Faith Determinations, REG–134974–12, 2012-47 I.R.B. 553 (Nov. 19, 2012)

Nye, Joseph S., Jr., *The Future of Power* (Public Affairs, New York, 2011)

One Hand Giveth, THE ECONOMIST, April 21, 2012, at 72

Ormerod, Paul, "Why Not Experiment?", in Michael Kinsley and Conor Clarke, eds., *Creative Capitalism* (Simon & Schuster, 2008)

Ortberg, John, *Who is This Man? The Unpredictable Impact of the Inescapable Jesus* (Zondervan, 2012)

Ostertag, Charles R., *We're Starting to Share Well with Others: Cross-Border Giving Lessons from the Court of Justice of the European Union*, 20 TUL. J. INT'L & COMP. L. 255 (2011)

Perry, Suzanne, *Charitable Deduction Faces a Fresh Challenge as Lawmakers Attempt to Close Deficit*, THE CHRONICLE OF PHILANTHROPY/TAX WATCH (Nov. 17, 2011), http://philanthropy.com/article/Charitable-Deduction-Faces-a/129815/

Perry, Suzanne, *White House Seeks to Spur Innovative Spending by Foundations*, THE CHRONICLE OF PHILANTHROPY/TAX WATCH (May 10, 2012), http://philanthropy.com/article/White-House-Seeks-to-Spur/131840/

Pozen, Robert C., *Why Not Venture-Capital Philanthropy?*, WALL STREET JOURNAL (June 3, 2012) (available online at http://online.wsj.com/article/SB10001424052702304840904577422243064-1379116.html)

Putnam, Robert D., et al., *Better Together: Restoring the American Community* (Simon & Schuster, 2003)

Putnam, Robert D., *Bowling Alone: The Collapse and Revival of American Community* (Simon & Schuster, 2000)

Raymond, Susan U., "It Really Is a Small World After All: Globalization and Philanthropy," in Raymond, Susan U., and Mary Beth Martin, eds., *Mapping the New World of American Philanthropy: Causes and Consequences of the Transfer of Wealth* (John Wiley & Sons, 2007)

Raymond, Susan, "The Tax Man Cometh: Should Nonprofits Pay?" in Raymond, Susan U., and Mary Beth Martin, eds., *Mapping the New World of American Philanthropy: Causes and Consequences of the Transfer of Wealth* (John Wiley & Sons, 2007)

Revenue Procedure 92-94, 1992-2 C.B. 507

Revenue Procedure 2011-33, 2011-25 I.R.B. 887

Revenue Procedure 2013-4, 2013-1 I.R.B. 126

Revenue Procedure 2013-8, 2013-1 I.R.B. 237

Revenue Ruling 63-252, 1963-2 C.B. 101

Revenue Ruling 64-182, 1964-1 C.B. 186

Revenue Ruling 66-79, 1966-1 C.B. 48

Revenue Ruling 73-440, 1973-2 C.B. 177

Revenue Ruling 74-574, 1974-2 C.B. 161

Revenue Ruling 75-65, 1975-1 C.B. 79

Revenue Ruling 78-95, 1978-1 C.B. 71.

Revenue Ruling 78-248, 1978-1 C.B. 154

Revenue Ruling 80-282, 1980-2 C.B. 178

Revised Model Nonprofit Corporation Act (Prentice Hall Law & Business, 1988)

Sachs, Jeffrey D., *Common Wealth: Economics for a Crowded Planet* (Penguin Books, 2008)

Sachs, Jeffrey D., *The End of Poverty: Economic Possibilities for Our Time* (Penguin Books, 2006)

Sachs, Jeffrey D., *The Price of Civilization: Reawakening American Virtue and Prosperity* (Random House, 2011)

Sanders, Michael I., and Celia Roady, "Private Foundations – Taxable Expenditures (Sec. 4945)," 474 Tax Mgmt. (BNA) Estates, Gifts, and Trusts, at A-1 (2011)

Saunders, Laura, *Charitable Deductions Under Fire*, WALL STREET JOURNAL (June 8, 2012)

Schenkelberg, Thomas J., and Virginia C. Gross, "Private Foundations – Distributions (Section 4942)," 880-2nd Tax Mgmt. (BNA) Estates, Gifts, and Trusts, at A-1 (2004)

Sen, Amartya, *Development as Freedom* (Alfred A. Knopf, 1999)

Sen, Amartya, "Rational Choice: Discipline, Brand Name, and Substance," in Fabienne Peter and H.B. Schmid, eds., *Rationality and Commitment* at 339 (Oxford University Press, 2007)

Shiller, Robert J., *Taxes Needn't Discourage Philanthropy*, NEW YORK TIMES (July 28, 2012) (http://www.nytimes.com/2012/07/29/business/if-raising-top-tax-rates-encourage-charitable-giving.html?_r=0)

Shoemaker, Ron, and Bill Brockner, *Public Charity Classification and Private Foundation Issues: Recent Emerging Significant Developments*, Continuing Professional Education Exempt Organizations Technical Instruction Program for Fiscal Year 2000 at 221(Internal Revenue Service)

Sierra Club, Inc. v. Commissioner, 86 F.3d 1526 (9th Cir. 1996)

Simpson, Steven D., *Tax Compliance for Tax-Exempt Organizations* (CCH, 2012 edition)

Spreading Gospels of Wealth, THE ECONOMIST, May 19, 2012, at 36

Stannard-Stockton, Sean, *Philanthropists' 'Soft Power' May Trump the Hard Pull of Purse Strings*, THE CHRONICLE OF PHILANTHROPY (April 18, 2010), http://philanthropy.com/article/article-content/65080/

Stokeld, Fred, *Exempt Organizations Must Report Payments Made to Americans Living Overseas, IRS Says*, 64 THE EXEMPT ORGANIZATION TAX REVIEW 243 (2009)

Sweetened Charity, THE ECONOMIST, June 9, 2012, at 29

A Taxonomic Tree of Philanthropy, CATALOGUE FOR PHILANTHROPY, http://www.cataloguefor-philanthropy.org/ma/2007/05_taxonomic_tree_of_philanthropy.html

U2, "Crumbs From Your Table," *How to Dismantle an Atomic Bomb*, (Universal Music Group, 2004)

The Unified Registration Statement: the Multi-State Filer Project, http://www.multistate-filing.org/ (web site last visited on March 3, 2013)

United States Code, Title 26 [Internal Revenue Code] – various sections

United States Department of the Treasury, Anti-Terrorist Financing Guidelines: Voluntary Best Practices for U.S.-Based Charities (available online at http://www.treasury.gov/resource-center/terrorist-illicit-finance/Pages/protecting-charities-intro.aspx) (web site last visited on March 3, 2013)

United States Department of the Treasury – Regulations – various provisions

United States Department of the Treasury, Examples of Program-Related Investments, 77 Fed. Reg. 23429 (proposed Apr. 19, 2012) (to be codified at 26 C.F.R. pt. 53)

United States Department of the Treasury, Reliance Standards for Making Good Faith Determinations, 77 Fed. Reg. 185 (proposed Sep. 24, 2012) (to be codified at 26 C.F.R. pt. 53)

United States Department of the Treasury, Risk Matrix for the Charitable Sector (available online at http://www.treasury.gov/resource-center/terrorist-illicit-finance/Pages/protecting-index.aspx) (web site last visited on March 3, 2013)

United States Department of the Treasury, Office of Foreign Assets Control, Specially Designated Nationals List, http://www.treasury.gov/resource-center/sanctions/SDN-List/Pages/default.aspx (web site last visited on March 3, 2013)

U.S. National Debt Clock, http://www.brillig.com/debt_clock/

Webster, Hugh K., "Tax-Exempt Organizations: Reporting, Disclosure and Other Procedural Aspects," 452 Tax. Mgmt. (BNA) Estates, Gifts, and Trusts, A-1 (2009)

Whittle, Dennis, "Markets for International Development," in Susan U. Raymond and Mary Beth Martin, eds., *Mapping the New World of American Philanthropy: Causes and Consequences of the Transfer of Wealth* (John Wiley & Sons, 2007)

Index

Also Published By the Council on International Law and Politics (http://www.cilpnet.org) and available on Amazon

International Business Transactions

Documents

edited by
Prof. Dr. Talia Einhorn and
Prof. Dr. Frank Emmert, LL.M.

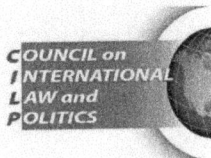

COUNCIL on
INTERNATIONAL
LAW and
POLITICS

After very encouraging feedback from their readers, Professors Einhorn and Emmert present an **updated and expanded 2nd edition** of their collection of materials on International Business Transactions. The volume now includes the 52 most widely used international conventions and model laws and is sure to become an indispensable tool for practitioners, students, and academics alike, a book to be kept nearby, a desk-copy for daily consultation. In addition to the most relevant international laws currently in force, the editors have included several important drafts, including the European Common Frame of Reference which will be the basis of the future European Civil Code. Practitioners are encouraged to consider these drafts and other model laws in this collection when developing their contracts for international business transactions.

The **key documents in the collection** include:
- United Nations Convention on Contracts for the International Sale of Goods (CISG)
- UCC Articles 1, 2, 4A, 5, 7 and 9
- Unidroit Principles of International Commercial Contracts
- EU Draft Common Frame of Reference
- Incoterms 2010
- Uniform Customs and Practice for Documentary Credit UCP600
- UNCITRAL Arbitration Rules
- ICC 850 Rules of Arbitration
- IBA Rules on Taking of Evidence in International Commercial Arbitration
- New York Convention on Recognition and Enforcement of Foreign Arbitral Awards

Prof. Dr. Talia Einhorn is Professor of Law at Ariel University Center, Department of Economics and Business Management and Senior Research Fellow at Tel Aviv University Faculty of Management. She has taught widely in Europe and the United States and is the author of many books and articles on comparative law, private international law, and international business law and arbitration.

Prof. Dr. Frank Emmert, LL.M. is the John S. Grimes Professor of Law and Director of the Center for International and Comparative Law at Indiana University Robert H. McKinney School of Law in Indianapolis. He has taught widely in Europe, the Middle East, and the United States and has published many books and articles in particular in the areas of European Union law, international business and trade law, and the transformation of legal systems towards democracy and rule of law.

The **Council on International Law and Politics** is a not-for-profit organization based in Chicago for the promotion of peaceful and fair political and trade relations between different peoples, countries, and regions around the world. Through research, publications, conferences, training, and other activities, CILP contributes to democracy, justice, human rights, rule of law, and economic and social development in Central- and South America, Africa, the Middle East, Eastern Europe, and Central and South-East Asia. Additional information is available at http://www.cilpnet.org.

COUNCIL on
INTERNATIONAL
LAW and
POLITICS

ISBN 9780985815622

90000 >

9 780985 815622

www.ingramcontent.com/pod-product-compliance
Lightning Source LLC
Chambersburg PA
CBHW080557220326
41599CB00032B/6508